PENGUIN BOOKS

AND THE PURSUIT OF HAPPINESS

Maira Kalman is an illustrator, author, and designer. She is the author of *And the Pursuit of Happiness* and *The Principles of Uncertainty*. She is the illustrator of Michael Pollan's *Food Rules* and the bestselling edition of William Strunk and E. B. White's *The Elements of Style*. Kalman's work is shown at the Julie Saul Gallery in Manhattan.

AND THE PURSUIT OF HAPPINESS

Maira Kalman

PENGUIN BOOKS

PENGUIN BOOKS

Published by the Penguin Group · Penguin Group (USA) Inc., 375 Hudson Street, New York, New York 10014, U.S.A. ·
Penguin Group (Canada), 90 Eglinton Avenue East, Suite 700, Toronto, Ontario, Canada M4P 2Y3 (a division of Pearson
Penguin Canada Inc.) · Penguin Books Ltd, 80 Strand, London WC2R 0RL, England · Penguin Ireland, 25 St. Stephen's
Green, Dublin 2, Ireland (a division of Penguin Books Ltd) · Penguin Books Australia Ltd, 250 Camberwell Road,
Camberwell, Victoria 3124, Australia (a division of Pearson Australia Group Pty Ltd) · Penguin Books India Pvt Ltd,
11 Community Centre, Panchsheel Park, New Delhi – 110 017, India · Penguin Group (NZ),
67 Apollo Drive, Rosedale, Auckland 0632, New Zealand (a division of Pearson
New Zealand Ltd) · Penguin Books (South Africa) (Pty) Ltd, 24 Sturdee Avenue,
Rosebank, Johannesburg 2196, South Africa

Penguin Books Ltd, Registered Offices:
80 Strand, London WC2R 0RL, England

First published in the United States of America by The Penguin Press, a member of Penguin Group (USA) Inc. 2010
Published in Penguin Books 2012

3   5   7   9   10   8   6   4   2

Copyright © Maira Kalman, 2010
All rights reserved

ILLUSTRATION CREDITS: *p. 211:* Courtesy of the Massachusetts Historical Society; *p. 270:* Brown Brothers,
ca. 1908 (detail), National Archives, photo no. 90-G-125-29; *pp. 318–319:* New York City Department of
Environmental Protection; *p. 327:* From *Marcel Proust: Letters to His Mother,* translated by George D. Painter.
By permission of The Random House Group, London; *p. 331:* Architect of the Capitol.
Original photographs by Rick Meyerowitz and by Maira Kalman

Most of the contents of this book first appeared as the author's online column
"And the Pursuit of Happiness" on the Web site of *The New York Times.*

My great thanks to the many generous people in government and community service who assisted in my excellent American
year. To the gracious people at the *New York Times,* especially David Shipley and Mary Duenwald. To Ann Godoff and all
the gracious people at Penguin Press. To Charlotte Sheedy, Peter Buchanan-Smith and Shawn Hasto. To Kika Schoenfeld,
for the title of this book. To Rick Meyerowitz for illumination on things past, present and future.
And, as always, this work is for Lulu Bodoni Kalman and Alexander Tibor Kalman.

ISBN 978-1-59420-267-4 (hc.)
ISBN 978-0-14-312203-6 (pbk.)

Printed in the United States of America

Designed by Peter Buchanan-Smith and Shawn Hasto
Design Intern, Devin Washburn

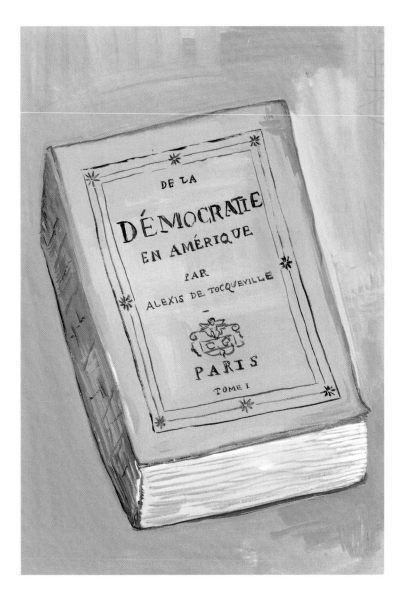

AND THE PURSUIT OF HAPPINESS

Maira Kalman

JANUARY

★

George Washington

The Inauguration. At Last.

HALLELUJAH.

The ANGeLs are SiNgiNG oN this gLoRious Day.

And we MORTALS, dRiViNG
white mountains and BLACK
industrial STUFF, Listen to
words from a Bach cantatA.

"Now is the time

And all I can

down to Washington, passing
Mountains of unidentified
Lorraine Hunt Lieberson sing

of GRACE."

The
HEART
is Racing.

say is Hallelujah.

HALLELUJAH FOR THE WALT WHITMAN
REST STOP ON THE NEW JERSEY TURNPIKE

WHERE THE PLASTIC FLOWERS IN THE
WOMEN'S RESTROOM LOOKED QUITE NOBLE.

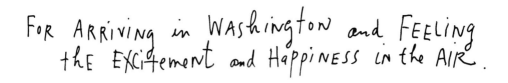

FOR ARRIVING in WASHINGTON and FEELING the EXCITEMENT and HAPPINESS in the AIR.

FOR the HATS in the Baptist Church.

At the Martin Luther King Day Service.

and
the
CHOIR
Singing
"WE
SHALL
OVERCOME."

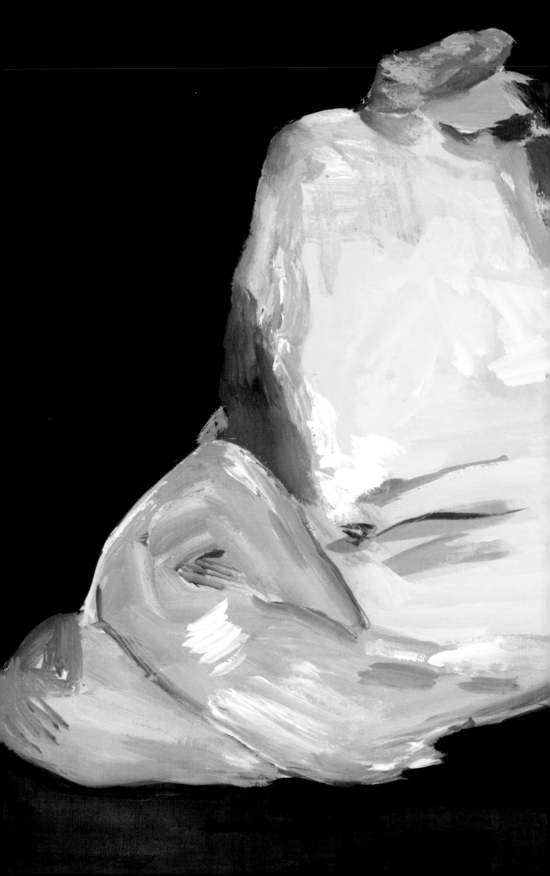

FOR the SMALL FRENCH PAINTING show at the National GALLERY and the ANTOINE VOLLON Painting of a MOUND of Butler with NOT ONE, BUT TWO EGGS.

FOR the GUARD
with the PERFECT
RED EYEBROWS
GUARDING the
PAINTINGS.

FOR JEFFERSON, IN thE
DECLARATION oF INDEPENDENCE
cHANging the woRds LIFE,
LiBERTy and the
PuRSuit of PRopERty to
the PuRSuit of HAppiNess.

HAPPINESS!

And for the SHOES
of the MAN portraying
JEFFERSON at the
MUSEUM of AMERICAN
History, who
spoke so confidently.

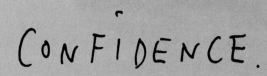

CONFIDENCE.

And while WE aRe at it,
HAlleLujAH FoR the
FORTUNY TEA GOWN
also on dispLay
iN the MUSEUM,

WHICH IS a TOTAL KNOCKOUT.

HALLELUJAH for KNOWLEDGE and FOR the HONOR
OF LANGUAGE and IDEAS. AND BOOKS.

FOR JEFFERSON'S GLORIOUS LIBRARY FULL OF
CICERO and SPINOZA and AESCHYLUS and
Thomas MORE and Books on BEES and TREES
and HARPSICHORDS ALL INTACT IN thE
LIBRARY OF CONGRESS.

FOR tHE STATELY RARE BOOKS READING ROOM
iN the LIBRARY:

AND foR the STATELY, PLUMP tASSEL hanging
on the RICH, CRIMSON cuRtaiN NEAR the peopLE
who WORK and STUDY tHERE.

And for the small worn velvet Bible Housed in the Rare Books Reading Room that Lincoln used For His inauguration and Obama used For His Inauguration.

Hallelujah For Being Allowed to Hold that Bible in My Hands.

Abraham Lincoln. Maira. Barack Hussein Obama.

Nice.

And a woman named Renata asked "Why on the Bible? Why not on the Constitution?" And I think That is a VERY Good Question.

But Now we are taking a SHORT BREAK FROM QUESTIONING.

RIGHT NOW, WE ARE OPTING FOR NAÏVETÉ.

HALLELUJAH FOR THE VAST SEA of NEARLY TWO MILLION PEOPLE HOLDING MADLY FLUTTERING FLAGS IN THE BRIGHT NOONDAY SUN.

FOR BEING SMART AGAIN.

AND SEXY AGAIN.

AND OPTIMISTIC AGAIN.

FOR the HELICOPTER ROARING UP
FROM BEHIND THE CAPITOL
NEXT TO THE JAPANESE PAGODA TREE.
A DOT IN THE SKY.

HALLELUJAH
FOR the
HOPE of a
NEW WORLD.

And the Japanese pagoda tree,
OBLIVIOUS to ALL the FUSS,
VAGUELY REMEMBERS THAT it
is ALSO KNOWN as the
CHINESE SCHOLAR TREE,

WHICH FLOWERS PROFUSELY IN Late SUMMER
OFFERING TO the LUCKY PERSON STANDING UNDER
IT A FRAGRANT DAPPLED REFUGE FROM the
NOONday SUN.

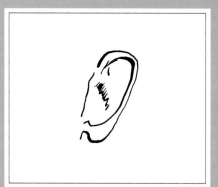

FEBRUARY

★

Abraham Lincoln

In Love With A. Lincoln

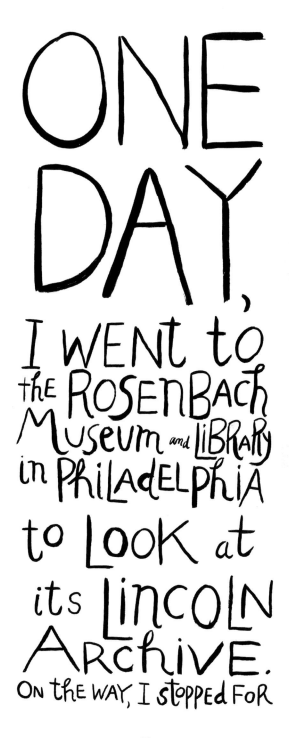

ONE
DAY,
I WENT to
the ROSENBACh
Museum and LiBRARy
in PhiLAdelphiA
to LooK at
its LiNCOLN
ARChiVE.
ON the WAY, I stopped FoR

Eggs.
I paid with a
Lincoln and two Washingtons.

WHEN I got to the LIBRARY I settled in and took Copious NOTES.

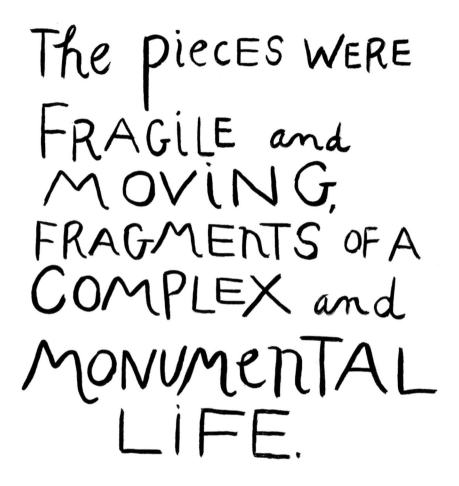

The pieces WERE FRAGILE and MOVING, FRAGMENTS OF A COMPLEX and MONUMENTAL LIFE.

LINCOLN
Red Folio

RED
FOLIO

Lincoln's Hat

Abraham

Lincoln

WA
A

Potosi Missouri

WAR DECLARED!!

Periwinkle
Blue
Paper
against
slavery

ABOLITION
DESPO
DespotismTIS
M.

MOURNING
Envelope A
NOTES IN HAT

a.l.

o-o-o-o
LiBERTY

Brady

M. Kalman
M. Kalman

A Lincoln

Penny

A Lincoln

When did they
make this
penny?

Emancipation Proclamation

1863

A.

A.

A.

A.
Doug
Wilson

A Lincoln
Brady

Lincoln Reminds Me of My cousin Azriel Azriel
as a teenager

Brady
Tenth Street and Broadway.

Brady's Portrait
Galleries

NATIONAL CEMETERY AT GETTYSBURG
November 19 1863

MUSIC
PRAYER
MUSIC
ORATION
MUSIC
REMARKs BY PRESIDENT
DIRGE
BENEDICTION

PRECISELY 10 o'clock a.m.

Lincoln
Martin Luther King. — The Lineage of Freedom
Barack Obama.

Shot April 14th – Good Friday
Thursday April 20 1865   Died April 15

FUNERAL

And

his COFFIN

14 th
15 th

His DEATH   MOURNING PIN.   OuR National Grief

THE COFFIN

GRIEF
grief

The more I read, the more entranced I became. Over 15,000 books have been written about Lincoln. I won't claim to have read them all. Or even any.

But it became clear as I tumbled into his world that he had a magnetic appeal.
I looked at images.

I LooKed
DEEP
INTO his
EYES
and
Found

that I
WAS
Falling
in
LOVE.

IN LOVE
with
A. LincolN.

Mrs. Maira Lincoln
requests the
pleasure of your company
at the Sunday Social

R. S. V. P.

punch   dainties

48

But let us begin the story.

It was a BEAUTIFUL Friday in April. The CIVIL WAR had ended JUST A FEW DAYS EARLIER. An unbearable BURDEN had BEEN Lifted.

Lincoln wanted to lighten their MOOD. A PLAY would BE the THING. BUT FATE had other Plans. HE WAS MURDERED—

SHOT in the HEAD with this PISTOL,

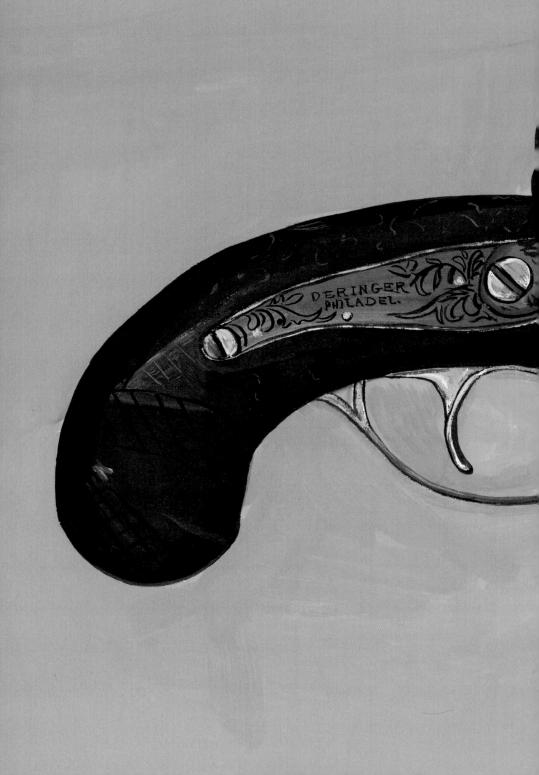

MURDERED WHILE HE WAS LAUGHING
AT A SILLY BRITISH COMEDY.

WHILE ROCKING in
this CHAIR.

HE WAS CARRIED
ACROSS the STREET,
and he DIED the
NEXT MORNING,

APRIL 15, 1865.
HE WAS 56 YEARS OLD.

How did it BEGIN?
HE WAS A GENIUS,
SPRUNG SEEMINGLY FROM NOWHERE.

BORN in this LOG CABIN
in KENTUCKY.

HE WAS LUCKY. HIS STEPMOTHER LOVED him LIKE CRAZY. And he ADORED HER. SHE LOOKS SO STERN. BUT SHE LET him DREAM and READ AS much AS he WANTED.

HE WENT TO SCHOOL FOR ONLY ONE YEAR. HE TAUGHT HIMSELF. EVERYTHING.

Subtraction of Long Mea

£	M	f	P
7	-1	3	10
44	2	5	16
21	-1	5	34
11	1	3	10

Subr

Y	f	f	B
48-0	1-2		
12-0	3-1		
36 0	10 1		
48-0	1-2		

# of Land Measure

A	R	P	40
12	1	10	
5	3	17	
6	1	33	
12	1	10	

A	R	P	40
17	3	17	
12	3	23	
4	3	34	
17	3	17	

a	r	p	40
28	1	7	
19	1	28	
8	3	19	
28	1	7	

# of Dry Measure

Ch	B	P	36 4
17	2	1	
10	9	3	
7	0	2	
17	2	1	

Ch	b	p	36 4
40	1	2	
16	5	1	
23	32	1	
30	7	2	

q	B	P	8 4
19	1	1	
12	7	2	
6	1	3	
19	1	1	

Abraham Lincoln
his hand and pen
he will be good but
god knows when

HAROLD HOLZER, the ELOQUENT LINCOLN AUTHORITY, told ME THAT WHEN LINCOLN WAS A LAD, hE WAS KICKED in the HEAd bY a MULE. SOME YEARS LATER, HE BECAME A LAWYER in SPRINGFIELD, Ill.

WE WENT TO VISIT his Land.

WE WENT STRAIGHT TO THE

CEMETERY and COLLECTED LEAVES.

WE STAYED in the MARY Todd LiNCoLN Room OF A LocAL BED-and-BREAKFAST.

IT WAS DUSTY and DREARY and I WAS SURE MARY WOULD have HAD oNE OF HER FAMOUS FITS IF SHE HAD STAYED THERE.

BUT WE WERE LUCKY.
AT BREAKFAST THE NEXT MORNING,
LINCOLN WALKED INTO THE ROOM.
A RETIRED MINISTER
who TRAVELS as A
LINCOLN PRESENTER.

THERE are
150 LINCOLN
PRESENTERS
ALL OVER
The
COUNTRY.

I have MET FOUR SO FAR.

Douglas Wilson is a RENOWNED Lincoln scholar who lives in GALESBURG, Ill. He told ME so much aBout LINCOLN.

Lincoln was Always SCRiBBLING NOTES And PUTTING them into His HAT. with His HAT on He WAS SEVEN FEET TALL.

How WAS he such A VISIONARY?

How could HE have WRITTEN so BRILLIANTLY?

How could he have UNDERSTOOD THAT the UNION MUST BE PRESERVED?

The South designed beautiful F L A G S,

but it was on the WRONG side of History.

The Civil War ground on.
The casualties were catastrophic,
totaling nearly a Million
and A HALF by WAR'S END.

We went to Gettysburg
and looked At the
numbeRed GRaVES.

8

on that BATTLEFIELD, LinColN gAVE ONE of history's gREAtEST SPEECHES, 272 WORDS Ending with

" goVERNMENT of the PEOPLE, by the PEOPLE, FOR the PEOPLE, shALL NOT PERISH FROM THIS EARTh."

WE ARE OVERWhELMED.

WE nEED SoMEThiNG TO EAT.

Lincoln DINER

At the
LINCOLN
DINER
there
ARE
ONLY TWO LINCOLN-Related
ITEMS ON THE MENU:
French Toast à la Lincoln
and
Italian Sub Lincoln-Style

(NO SUBSTITUTIONS).

THE ROTATING CAKE DISPLAY DOES NOT
include LINCOLN'S FAVORITE, THE white
CAKE Mary baked for him.

Did he LOVE his wife?
Opinions differ. MayBE.

DESPITE HER EXPLOSIVE TEMPER and out-of-CONTROL SPENDING, he VALUEd HER. Did he HAVE nicknames FOR HER? LittLE Dumpling? Plumpy? WhAt did sHE cALL HiM? Linky? PoKEY? MAYBE NOt.

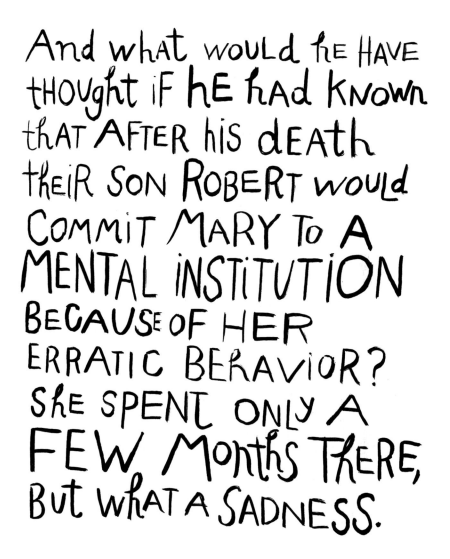

And what would he HAVE thought if hE had known thAT AFTER his dEAth thEiR SON ROBERT would Commit MARY To A MENTAL INSTiTUTiON BECAUSE OF HER ERRATIC BEhAViOR? ShE SPENT ONLY A FEW MONthS THERE, But whAT A SADNESS.

WHAT ELSE SHOULD you KNOW?

HE LOVED PEOPLE · REALLY.

HE had A DOG named FIDO.
I think FIDO WAS CROSS-EYED.

HE LOVED APPLES.

Cox PIPPIN
WHITE PIPPIN
RUSSET
WINESAP
BENONI
STRIPED
GILLIFLOWER
SEEK-NO-FURTHER
PECK'S PLEASANT
DUCHESS OF OLDENBURG

And he loved Music.

He loved Mozart. Lincoln loved Mozart! Especially "The Magic Flute."

And he loved Shakespeare. Especially "Macbeth."

And he MAY HAVE ENJoyed THE

EVER-SO-DELICATE
Plomping
ARound the
STAGE of
LauRa Le CLAIRE,
the
POPULAR
BALLERINA.

And WHAT ELSE WAS happening
ARound the WORLD?
A few years before LiNcoLN
issued the Emancipation
PRoclamation, CzaR Alexander II
oF RvSSIA issued his own
proclamation FReeiNg the SERFS.

And while the CZaR had Lavish Banqvets
wHere gvESTs ENjoYed SoufFLÉS à la rEINE,
LoBsTeR à la pARISiENNE, CANapÉs oF ORTOLAN,
CAssoLettE pRiNCESSE, BomBes gLACÉEs and
much MORE, the LiNcolNs had tHEIR
FANcy EVeNts wHere they ENjoyed
   OYSTeR STEW, BEEF à la ModE,
   VEAL MaLaKoFF, pâté of dvcK eN geLÉE,
ORNAMeNTAL PyRamids of NOvgAT and
caRamel with FANcy CReam CANdy,
tARtE à la NelsoN, chaRLotte à la Russe,
CRème glacèe napoLitaiNe and, OF coURSE,
        FANcy SMALL CAKES.

And what was happening in JAPAN?
Emperor Komeñ, attended by
hundreds of servants and
CONCUBINES, was issuing
his OWN PROCLAMATION
saying FOREIGNERS (BARBARIANS)
were NOT Welcome.
KEEP THEM AWAY.

And what of HIS HAT
Compared to LINCOLN'S?
And his BEARD
COMPARED to the
CZaR'S MUSTACHE?
ALL of this history makes
me want to EMBRACE
Lincoln and BRing him
into MY WORLd.
I imagine us WALKing
ARound NEW YORK.
WE WOULd go STRAIGHT To the
MUSEUM of MODERN ART. maybe
WE WOULd look at SELF-PORTRAITS BY

FRIDA KAHLO.

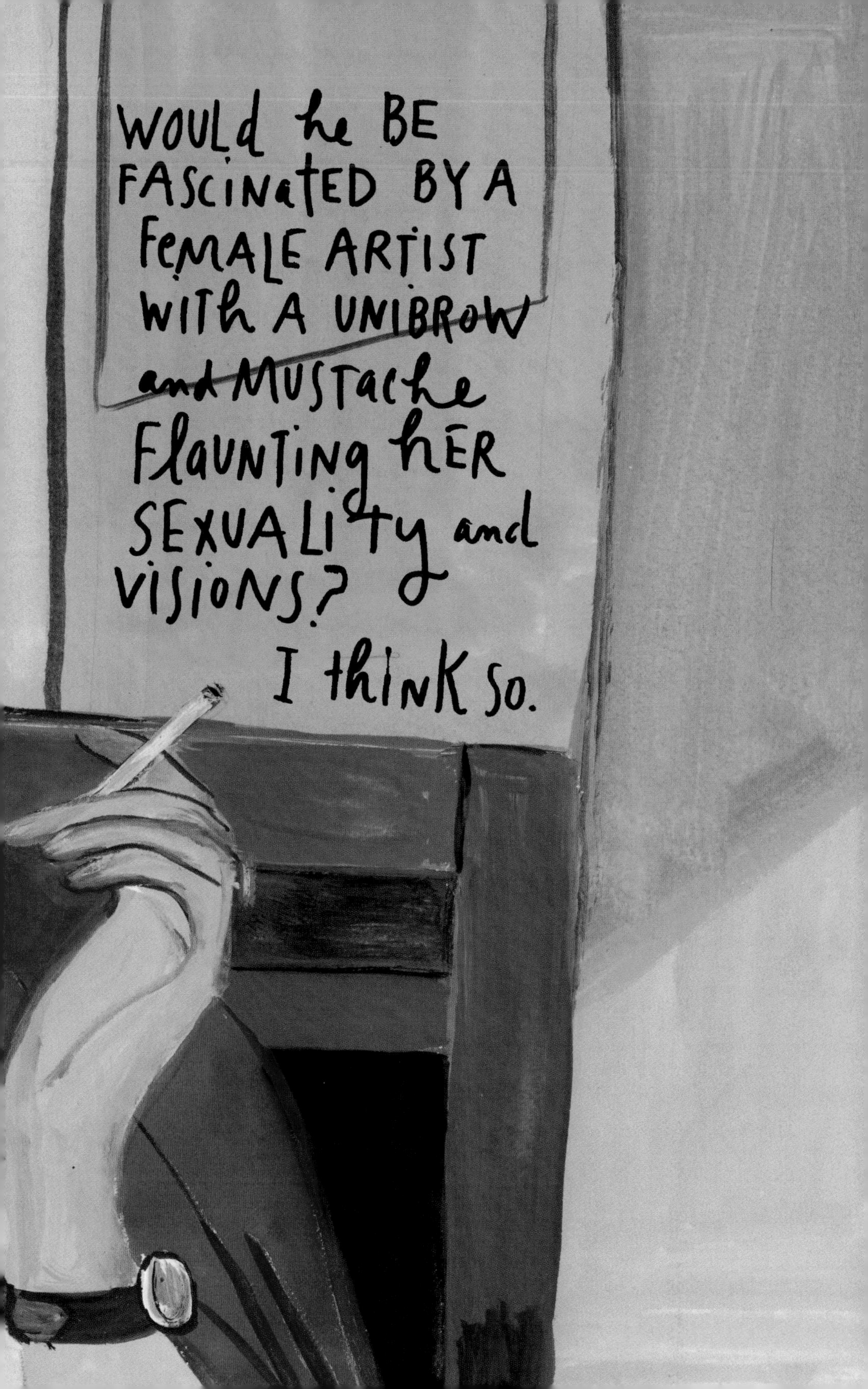
Would he BE FASCINATED BY A FEMALE ARTIST WITH A UNIBROW and MUSTACHE Flaunting HER SEXUALITY and VISIONS?
I think so.

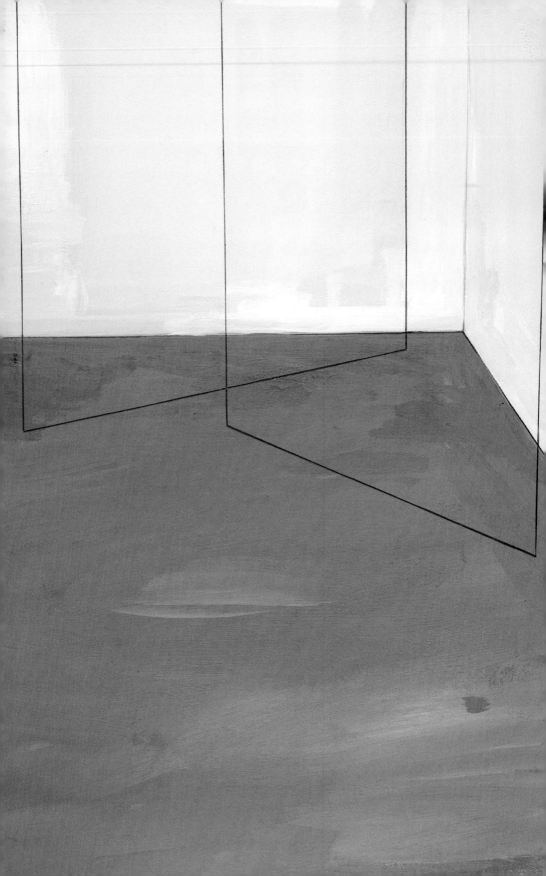

IF thERE WAS an EXhiBiT oF FRed SandbacK SculptuRES, WE WOULD RACE OVER To THAT.

HE WOULD NOT BE DISMISSIVE OF This PHILOSOPHER OF STRiNG and SpACE. BUT he Might MaKe a jOKE ABOUT ART.

BAKED PO

THEN WE WOULD GO TO THE
BAKED POTATO KING FOR A BITE.

TATO KING

NO FANCY RESTAURANT FOR US.
AFTER THAT WE WOULD go HOME.

I WOULD CONFESS TO him THAT I would LOVE to LIVE

in the LINCOLN MEMORIAL. JUST a SIMPLE COT in thE CENTER of the SPACE.

I would MAKE MY BED and SWEEP. DRINK teA. My nEatNESS and HAPPY ASPECT WOULD AMUSE him. In the EVENING I would EMBROIDER his WORDS ONTO FABRIC.

WORDS thAT SEEM SO APT TodAY.

The Occasion is Piled High with Difficulty. As our Case IS NEW, so We Must Think Anew, and Act Anew. We MUST DISENThrall Ourselves, and THEN WE SHALL SAVE ouR COUNTRy.

A. Lincoln
1862

MARCH

★

Mary Todd Lincoln

In 1535, Sir Thomas More, the author of "UTOPIA," a novel about a perfect society, Had a Disagreement with King Henry VIII. Henry had him Beheaded.

SO MUCH FOR a PERFECT SOCIETY.

SIX YEARS LATER, MARGARET PLANTAGENET POLE, the Countess of SALISBURY, didn't quite SEE EYE to EYE

with HENRY. So he had her BEheaded. Not long after that, some of the SALISBURYS said, "LET'S GET OUT of HERE."

THEY WENT to AMERICA.

A Few hundRed YEARS LATER, A BeheAding
CRAZE SWEPT FRANCE. ALEXIS de TOCQUEVILLE'S
PaRENTS, AWAiTing EXECUTIoN, WERE SPARED the
guilloTiNE and FReed. This mAde a deep ImpRession
on ALEXIS, who decided in 1830 to SAil To
AMERiCA and OBSERVE FiRSThand this NEW thing
CALLed DEMOCRACY.

HE spent a YEAR TRAVELING and INTERVIEWING
PEOPLE, then wROTE A BOOK, APTLY TITLED
"DE LA DÉMOCRATIE EN AMÉRIQUE."

His WRITING WAS FILLED with ASTUTE REFLECTIONS:
"IF ONE ASKED ME To whAT do I think oNE MUST
PRINcipALly aTTRIBUTE The SINGuLaR pROSpERITY
and gROWING FORCE of tHIS PEOPLE,

I would ANSWER
thAT it is to The
SUPERIORITY
oF ITS
WOMEN."

oh, TocqueviLLE,
you'Re the MAN.

I think he would have liked Rebecca Salisbury of Massachusetts, an arbiter of taste and a fine figure of a woman.

Rebecca married Daniel Waldo. Daniel Waldo had a relative named

DANIEL WALDO who WAS ONE of the FEW MEN in the REVOLUTIONARY WAR who lived long ENough to be photographed.

He FELL down a flight of STAIRS at the Age of 101. His WiFe died in a MENTAL INStitution AFTER 50 YEARS oF BEING CRAZY.

I wonder, WHAT CONSTITUTED CRAZY in those DAYS? VERY SAD.

THE SALISBURYS WERE A PRODUCTIVE NEW ENGLAND LOT.
DR. J.H. SALISBURY TENDED TO THE WOUNDED DURING THE CIVIL WAR.

Broiled
SALISBURY
STEAK DINNER
whipped potatoes, peas.
chicken noodle soup + peach cobbler

THREE COURSES·APPET

Today, in Vermont, if you like,

HE BELIEVED THAT EATING VEGETABLES MADE YOU SICK.
HIS CLAIM TO FAME WAS THE SALISBURY STEAK.

you CAN BUY a SALISBURY steak.

But that is not why we went to
Newfane, VT. We went to observe,
as Tocqueville did, the essence of
American democracy.

Town Meeting.

One person. One vote.
The purest form of Equal Representation.
For hundreds of years the residents
of small towns across New England
have gathered together in their
meeting halls on the appointed day
to vote on issues.

The Meeting hALL is No VERSAILLES.
It is SPARE and hoNEST.

I imagiNE it wiLL SooN be FiLLed with
aLL Kinds of chARACTERS VENtiNg thEiR FuRY
aBouT PERCEiVEd injuSTices. I Am ExciTEd.

But no. People speak their mind with grace and civility. They listen with RESPECT.

The ENTERPRISE is BASED on trust. Will you trust what your neighbors tell you? Will you trust that the system will work and people will be FAIR? I have my PARANOID, PESSIMISTIC side. But who doesn't?

Town Clerks are voted in by AUSTRALIAN (SECRET) BALLOT.

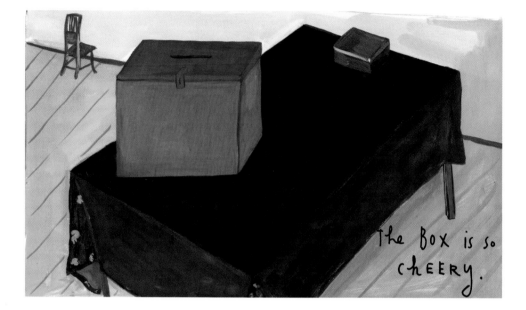

The BOX is so cheery.

But most things are discussed and people say AYE or NO.

Motion to Repair the FLOOR of the SENIOR CITIZENS' CENTER.
The AYES have it. So moved.

Motion to decommission the NUCLEAR power plant.
The AYES have it. So moved.

Motion to buy a new BACKHOE. A LOT of discussion.
Finally the AYES have it. So moved.

And then a REALLY IMPORTANT MOTION.

Motion to RECESS FOR LUNCH. The AYES have it. So moved.

WE EAT MACARONI and cheese. BARBECUE CHICKEN.
CORN bREAD. COFFEE CAKE. BROWNIES. the WORKS.

Sitting together. Democrats and Republicans.
Atheists and Believers. Can this system work?
I am filled with optimism. A sunny room.
A pleasant meal. Convivial conversation.

That's the kind of government
I like.

You are never too young to learn
about the DEMOCRATIC PROCESS.
EMPOWERMENT. COMPROMISE. DEFEAT.
PERSEVERANCE.

AT P.S. 47 in the BRONX, the
third-, fourth- and fifth-grade
student council meeting is in session.

THE PRESIDENT is commanding.
THE ISSUES are PRESSING.

WHAT COLOR CLOTHES
to WEAR FOR COLOR DAY?
THE STUDENTS VOTE
FOR WHITE.

HOW to HELP THE
COMMUNITY WITH
RECYCLING?
THEY WILL BRING
CANS AND BOTTLES
to A LOCAL CHURCH.

WHAT FUN EVENT
to PLAN FOR
SPECTACULAR FRIDAY,
AN EFFORT to
COMBAT
TRUANCY?

TALENT CONTEST? BAKE SALE? SPELLING BEE?
I love the Spelling Bee idea, but spelling is not
everyone's idea of FUN. BESIDES, my vote doesn't count.

THERE IS a
DISCUSSION of
Being Role Models
and the Responsibility
of it all. SOME
children couldn't
TAKE the PRESSURE,
So they QUIT.
SOME have FOUND
  it BORING.

Not this girl. Not AT. ALL.

BACK to SPECTACULAR FridAy. VOTes are Counted. THEN tHERE iS a MOTiON to RECESS FoR PiZZA and SoDA. And though the SPELLiNg BEE did NOT WIN, and I am a BiT DEJECTed, WE all sit together as FRiENDS and CHAT aBout OUR LiVES.

SO MOVED.

APRIL

★

John Adams

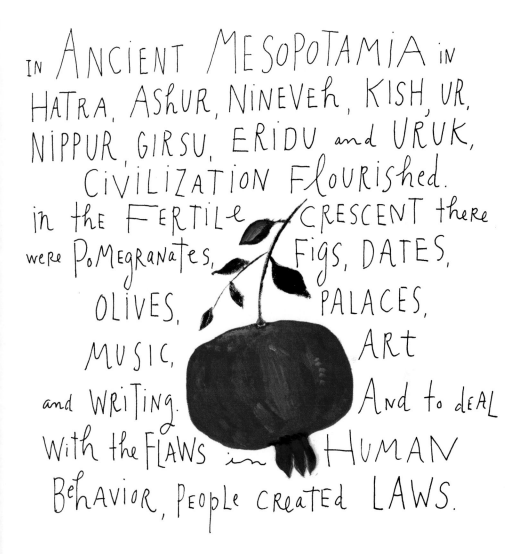

IN ANCIENT MESOPOTAMIA IN HATRA, ASHUR, NINEVEH, KISH, UR, NIPPUR, GIRSU, ERIDU and URUK, CIVILIZATION FLOURISHED. in the FERTILE CRESCENT there were POMEGRANATES, FIGS, DATES, OLIVES, PALACES, MUSIC, ART and WRITING. And to dEAL With the FLAWS in HUMAN BEhAVIOR, PEOPLE CREATED LAWS.

JUSTICE OVER OPPRESSION.

My FAVORITE LAW is Nº. 21:
IF A MAN SEVERS the
NOSE of ANOTHER
MAN with  A
K
N
i
F
E,
hE MUST pay HiM
two-thirds of a MiNa
(40 sheKels) of SiLVER.
LATER, with HAMMURabi, there WAS
AN EYE FoR aN EYE.

THERE are MANY other Kinds of LAWS.

The LAWS of NATURE. The LAWS of MATHeMATICS. The LAWS of the JUNGLE. The Laws of PESACh BERMAN, my FATHER.

Law no 1. No Singing at the DINNER TABLE.

Law no 2. Do good deeds FoR STRANGERS, BuT BEWARE oF RELATIVES.

AMERICA's FOUNDERS SAW to IT thAT WE would BE a NATION of LAWS.

I go to WAShington to visit the SUPREME COURT.

My BLACK UMBReLLA RESTS against the YELLOW WALL of the HoteL RoOM. WeLL, I think, No Need to ever LEAVE this room. And YET.

OuTside, iT is A MAD FRENZy oF PiNK.
THE MAGNOLIAS aRE BURSTING OPEN.

THE CHERRY BLOSSOMS aRE Clouds
of FLUTTERING PINK.

And in front of the SUPREME COURT FACADE
that states "EQUAL JUSTICE UNDER LAW"

EQUAL JUSTICE UNDER LAW

STANDS a WOMAN in a
SHOCKING-PINK COAT.

PINK it is.

Inside it is ALL Polished wood and MARBLE and Red VELVet DRapES and DECORUM and HISTORY, and EVERYthing You would Want in a

SUPREME COURT.

In the CouRt the LawyeRs aRe ARguing CASES that I Kind of understand. BUT NOT REALLY.

NOT REALLY is PUTTING it MILdLY.
BUT THAT is Not the PoINT.

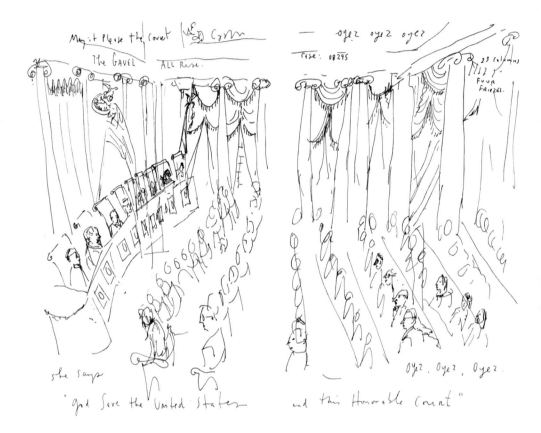

IT IS ALL ABOUT LANGUAGE,
the Language of DISSENT

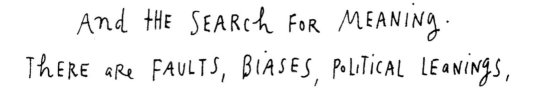

AND THE SEARCH FOR MEANING.
THERE ARE FAULTS, BIASES, POLITICAL LEANINGS,

WELLCOME to the Supreme Court of the U.S.

Due Process
Broad Language

DIFFERENCES OF PHILOSOPHY.
UNAVOIDABLE. THEY ARE HUMAN BEINGS.

But theRE is someThing ELSE. It is FRiendly.
THERe is a SeNSE of WeLL-BeiNg and HARMoNy.
No miseRable clerKs scuRRying aRound.
They seem to Love it HERE. HeaR, HeaR!
I LiKe the pEople.
The PuBLiC INFORMatioN OFFiCER.
the CouRT MARShaL who gETs To
BANg the GAVEL and say
" OYEZ OYEZ OYEZ."

The CouRT CLERK who WEARS
a DAPPER MoRNiNg Suit.
WE discuss tRadiFion and
the INtelLectuaL exchange of ideAS.
He tells me, "In the couRt,
youR adveRSARy is Not youR ENeMy."
How do people handLe that?
I wonDeR.

And then I meet Ruth Bader Ginsburg.
She is PETITE and Elegant.
I think, MOVE over Jane Austen as my imaginary Best Friend
Forever. Make Room for Ruth Bader Ginsburg, who would
have gone to my high school for MUSIC, if her parents
had let her. whose favorite
artist is MATISSE.
(I rest my CASE.)

who went on to study the LAW because she wanted to combat the FORCES of INJUSTICE (McCarthyism) and gRaduated tiEd foR fiRST in heR CLASS at COLUMBIA Law School, but could not get HIRed as a LAWYER.

We talk about MAKING DECISIONS and DOING the BEST
you CAN and THEN MOVING ON. How iLLNESS is
A DISTRACTION THAT MUST BE DEFEATED
So You CAN FOCUS ON the
REAL WORK.

I learn that her husband makes a SUBLIME grand
Marnier cake. (recipe needed.) That she ADORES
the OPERA, which is FASCINATING to ME, BECAUSE it
is ALL MADNESS, MURDER and UNControLLed PASSION.

the OPPOSITE of LAW.

But MayBE not.

She SHOWS ME HER CLOSET of ROBES and DOILY COLLARS.
SOME of THEM COME FROM a SHOP in PARIS.

I think I could go to PARIS, buy a Robe
and collar and wear it while I draw
in my studio. It might give me self-confidence.
I could throw around phrases like PRIMA FACIE
OR CERTIORI. WHY NOT?

Here is Ruth as a young girl with her cousin.
This is a girl who knew what was what.
Who had an arc of optimism in her.

May it Please the Court, it is time For Lunch.

Lunch 01669 is not the greatest Lunch I have ever had, but I cherish my NUMBER ticket.

Then I Leave.

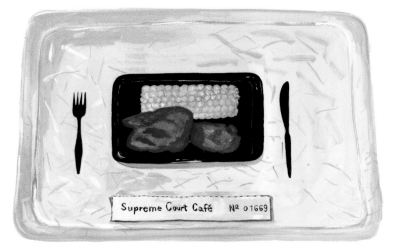

Supreme Court Café   № 01669

Skipping down the steps, still Aglow with Love of the Law and People, I come to an abrupt STOP.
There are a handful of People loudly protesting male circumcision.
They want to change the Law. They want it to be ILLEGAL.

Well, I think, EVERYONE has a Right to
Be Heard. But then I think, what a
Bunch of Schnooks. So much for
my being openminded and believing
everyone should have his Day in Court.

Then I visit the National gallery,
where there are plenty of naked Men, but I look at
a Bust of Voltaire in a magnificent wig. He also
studied the Law, but found it boring and gave it Up.

He had an AFFAIR
with the
BRILLIANT physicist
and Mathematician
Émilie Le Tonnelier,
the MARQUISE
du CHÂTELET.
She translated
NEWTON'S
"PRINCIPIA
MATHEMATICA".

I return to the court to hear
Justice Ginsburg speak to law
students. And in answer to the
question "How does it feel to be
the only woman on the court?"
she answers simply,
"Lonely."

I think about LONELINESS and Accomplishment and COURAGE. Sojourner TRUTH was sold to this MAN and then that MAN and then another MAN, and was finally freed. She fought for justice her entire life.

In court she fought for her son's freedom. And won.

And there is Susan B. Anthony.
She also challenged the
law because she
believed women
should vote.
I visit
Rochester,
where she
lived
and is
buried.
She was
quite beautiful
and
determined.

I look at her BRUSH and comB.
She loved beautiful things.

She Really Existed.
She ended up Looking VERY STERN.
And Why NOT?

ON the walls of hER Rooms aRe photos of women who fought foR women's Rights. My favoRite is DR. Hanna Rydh, an archaeologist and suffRagist.

She KNEW how to PROTEST.
She KNEW how to dRESS.

At Ease

"I do solemnly swear that I will support and defend
the Constitution of the United States against all
enemies, foreign and domestic; that I will bear
true faith and allegiance to the same; and that I
will obey the orders of the president of the United
States and the orders of the officers appointed over
me, according to regulations and the Uniform Code
of Military Justice. So help me God."

—Soldier's Oath

IT IS MEMORIAL DAY.
OUR NATION IS AT WAR.
THERE ARE WARS that WERE CoNSidERed
GOOD WARS. NECESSARY WARS.
THE REVOLUTIONARY WAR and the
CIVIL WAR and WORLD WAR II.
THE COUNTRY WAS UNITED.

✴

And NOW? THE PERIL IS REAL
BUT ELUSIVE.
IRAQ. IRAN. AFGHANISTAN.
PAKISTAN. NoRTh KOREA.
CAN THERE EVER BE PEACE ON
THIS PLANET?
No. ABSOLUTELY NOT.

MAY

★

Andrew Jackson

And then I come Home and look at a photo of dear Eleanor Rouseveltwearing an improbable yet wonderful HAT. Where does courage come from?
I call my aunt in Israel. She is 92. And I ask her, "What is the most important thing?" And she answers, "Self-confidence."

FORT CAMPBELL, KY.

EVERYONE IS BEAUTIFUL.
EVERYONE MAKES YOU PROUD.
EVERYONE BREAKS YOUR HEART.

THE SOLDIERS OF THE SCREAMING EAGLES,
the 101st AIRBORNE DIVISION, ARE
TRAINING FOR DEPLOYMENT.

THEY ARE LEARNING how to RAPPEL
OUT OF CHINOOK HELICOPTERS, UPSIDE DOWN
(AUSSIE STYLE), ENABLING THEM TO SHOOT A RIFLE.

THEY ARE TRAINING IN A MOCK ARAB VILLAGE.
I HAVE TO REMIND MYSELF THAT IT IS NOT A
MOVIE SET. THEY WALK TOGETHER IN A PORCUPINE
FORMATION, RIFLES MOVING AT ALL TIMES.

THEY DON'T GO THROUGH DOORS.
DOORWAYS ARE DEADLY and CALLED
"FATAL FUNNELS."
THEY BLAST THROUGH A WALL TO SURPRISE
THE ENEMY. AND OFTEN THE ENEMY
HAS SURPRISED THE SOLDIERS BY SURROUNDING
HIMSELF WITH WOMEN AND CHILDREN.

THEY WILL GO TO IRAQ and AFGHANISTAN TO FIGHT. THEY WILL FIGHT.

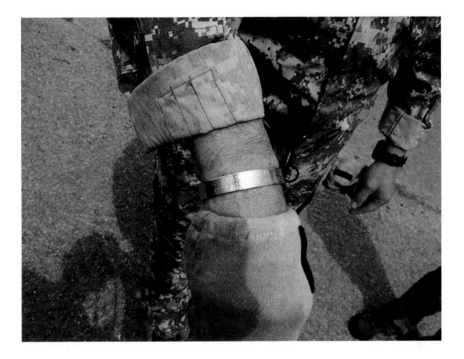

AND WHEN THEY RETURN HOME, THEY WILL WEAR BRACELETS HONORING THEIR FALLEN COMRADES IN ARMS.

The MONOTONOUS EXPANSES OF DRAB BUILDINGS LEAVE YOU YEARNING FOR COLOR.

THE CHERRY PIE on the RED TRAY in the BASE CAFETERIA IS A MOMENTARY BRIGHT SPOT.

And ONCE in a WHILE there is EVEN HUMOR.
the M.R.E.'s MEALS - READY To EAT - COME with
A HOOAH! POWER BAR.

HOOAH IS AN EXCLAMATION USED FOR EVERYTHING.
FOR YES and NO
and YOU CAN'T BE SERIOUS and IT WILL BE DONE and
I DON'T KNOW and GIVE ME A BREAK.

U.S. Central
Standard Time

Iraq
Time

THE WIVES WAIT FOR THEIR HUSBANDS IN SNUG BEIGE HOUSES — Like this Model HoME, with A CHILLING CLOCK DISPLAY.

The SPOUSES TAKE CARE OF the KIDS and WORK and PULL UP THEIR SOCKS. A WOMAN SAYS to ME OF her HUSBAND on his Fourth TOUR in IRAQ, "I WALK WITH A HERO." And IT is TRUE.

THE HUMVEES WILL BE REPLACED with MRAPS (MINE-RESISTANT, AMBUSH-PROTECTED VEHICLES) BECAUSE there ARE So MANY I.E.D.'s (IMPROVISED EXPLOSIVE DEVICES). The BODY ARMOR is much LIGHTER than it USED To BE. EVERY Soldier has a RADIO HeadsET.

And the HORRORS of WAR? And the TERROR? And the RUINED LiVES? ON Both SiDES. Who can hANDLE the CONTRADictiON S?

And if you NEED TO GEt OFF the BASE?
You caN go to NASHVILLE and HEAR SOME MUSIC.
And SEE TULIP POPLAR TRees that aRe So LOVELY,

and visit the
  HERMITAGE, hoME
OF ANDREW JACKSON,
who FOUGHT 14 DUELS,
BECAUSE he WAS A NUT FOR
HONOR OR FIGHTING OR BOTh.

THEN You CAN go HAVE BISCUITS and
PONDER WAR and PEACE WHILE
SITTING in a
FRIVOLOUS
and
SAFE
CHAIR
AT A
LOCAL
BARBECUE
JOINT.

AND SOLDIER No. 53?

The PENTAGON, ARLINGTON, VA.

"I am an American soldier....
I serve the people of the United States....
I will always place the mission first.
I will never accept defeat.
I will never quit.
I will never leave a fallen comrade....
I am a guardian of freedom and the American
way of life."

—Soldier's Creed

The three-hole punch has character. It punches three HOLES COUNTLESS times a day to FILL Binders with the Countless FORMS and

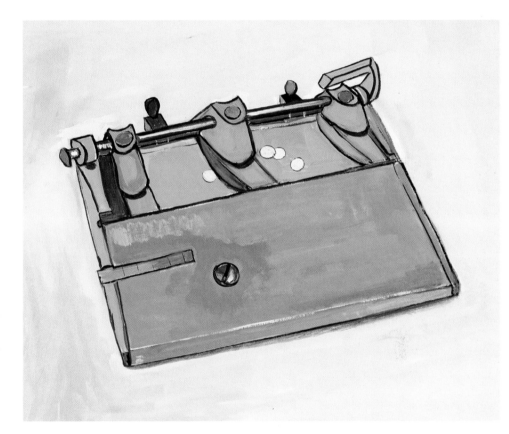

Documents and RULES and Regulations and Procedures. This is A BIG COMPANY.

THERE ARE 24,000 people who work at the PENTAGON. They ARE SMART and SERIOUS and REPRESENT their COUNTRY with HONOR.

People ZIP through endLESS, ENDLESS CORRidors, STRiding PAST IN SNAPPY UNiFORMS.

I ZIP past DEFENSE SECRETARY ROBERT GATES'S OFFICE and COME to A HALT. ON his WALL is A PAINTING

OF the WORLD WAR II B-17 BOMBER KNOWN as the FLYING FORTRESS.

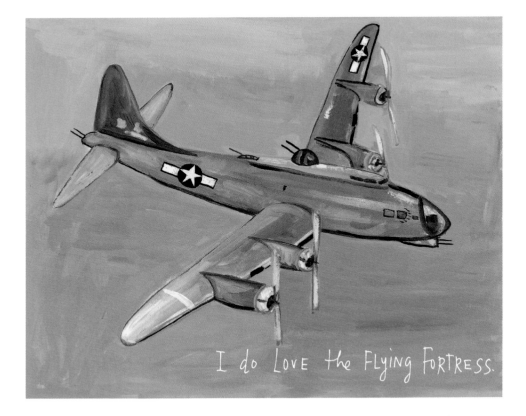

I do LoVE the FLying FoRtRESS.

BUT I WONDER, why does the Building
HAVE to BE AS BLAND and AS SOULLESS
        AS A HOSPITAL?
HAVE they NOT SEEN ANY JAMES Bond
    MOVIES? WOULD it KILL them to
        HAVE SOME STYLE?
CAN'T they BORROW PAINTINGS FROM
        the SMITHSONIAN? AND I
    don't MEAN BATTLE PAINTINGS.
HOW ABOUT SOME CEZANNES?
    I KNOW they would BE SAFE.

                ✭

MORE than THREE MILLION PEOPLE
        WORK FOR the MILITARY.
ABOUT A MILLION and a HALF aRE ON
ACTIVE DUTY, AND 200,000 OF those
            ARE WOMEN.

BY LAW, WOMEN CANNOT ENGAGE in
    ACTIVE COMBAT, BUT they STILL go
INTO HARM'S WAY. DRIVING CONVOYS.
        FLYING HELICOPTERS.

KATHERINE ABBOT IS A
COLONEL. FOUR RANKS AWAY
FROM A FOUR-STAR GENERAL.
SHE HAS FIVE CHILDREN AND WEARS
FATIGUES. SHE KNOWS SHE IS DOING THE RIGHT THING.
AND I ADMIRE HER.

ARMED FORCES HOSTESS

AIR FORCE   ARMY

INFORMATION
AND
SERVICES

MARINES   NAVY

MONDAY - FRIDAY
9:30AM - 2:30PM

COAST GUARD

ASSOCIATION

Is there such a thing as a PERSON BORN
with a MILITARY GENE?

Don't WE NEED Both the WARRIORS and
the ARTISTS on this PLANET?

WHAT IF I WERE IN the ARMY?
Apart FROM AN IMPECCABLY MADE BED,
I CAN'T imagine whAT ELSE I could do.

FLy a CHINOOK? PEEL POTATOES?
OR MAYBE BE A HOSTESS.

September 11, 2001

FINALLY WE GO OUTSIDE the BUILDING
to SEE the PRECISE SPOT WHERE ON
SEPT. 11 FLIGHT 77 RAMMED
INTO the WALL at 500 m.p.h.
KILLING 189 PEOPLE.

People in the MILITARY TeLL ME
YOU CANNOT have PEACE without WAR.
"IF WE don't FIGHT the ENEMY thERE,
WE WILL BE FIGHTING them HERE."

And the PRICE?

Blood AND TREASURE.

FULL STOP.

JUNE

★

Thomas Jefferson

Time Wastes Too Fast

I would like to
Tell you EVERYThiNG.

About the SILENCE aRound
the PYRaMids of GIZA.

ABOUT the CRAZY RUBBERY
Long-Beaked Echidna.

About why being in Le Corbusier's Ronchamp Chapel is a RELIGIOUS EXPERIENCE.

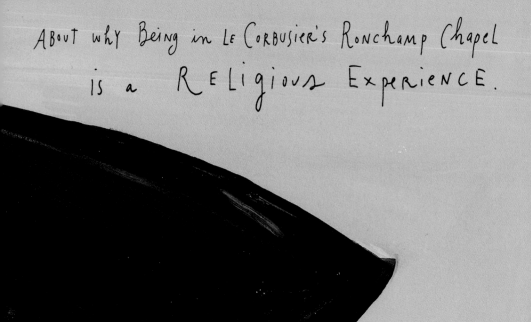

About the KATSURA IMPERIAL VILLA outside Kyoto
and dRiNKiNG POMEGRANATINIS with my FRiENDS
MR. AHARONI and MR. Noey.

I would tell you all this because he was a RENAISSANCE MAN and would have been FASCINATED by all of these things. MORE than MOST people.

But there is NO TIME. NO TIME.

IF you WANT to UNDERSTAND this COUNTRY and its people and whAT it MEANS to be OPTIMISTIC and COMPLEX and TRAGIC and WRONG and COURAGEOUS, You Need to go to his HOME in VIRGINIA. MONTICELLO.

IMAGINE YOU ARE INVITED.
I WAS.

Th: Jefferson
presents his compliments to
Maira Kalman
and requests the favour of her company
to dinner on Wednesday   next
at half after three oclock

The favour of an answer is requested

yes!

JUNE 1, 2009

MONTICELLO

Thomas Jefferson WAS A SCiENTiST, PHiLOSoPHER, STATESMAN, ARChiTECT, MVSiCiAN, NATVRALiST, ZooLoGiST, BoTANiST, FARMeR, BiBLioPHiLE, INVeNToR, WiNE CoNNoiSSeVR, MATHEMaTiCiAN and and...

HE WAS GoVeRNoR of ViRGiNiA, SECRetaRy of STATE, MiNiSteR to the CouRT oF LOUiS XVI, ViCE PRESidENT and thEN PRESidENT of the UNited StATES, iNitiaToR of the LOUiSiANA PuRChASE and its ExploRation by LEWiS and CLARK.

You waLK into the PALLAdiAN house that he designed and redesigned, with the tRiple sash windows that he invented and you immediately appreciate the bReadth of his cuRiosiTY. WHAT ELSE?

HE VEHEMENTLY BELIEVED IN SEPARATION OF CHURCH AND STATE. HE FOUNDED THE UNIVERSITY OF VIRGINIA, ONE OF THE FIRST NON-RELIGIOUS COLLEGES IN THE COUNTRY.

THERE ARE A FEW MORE LITTLE THINGS. HE WROTE THE DECLARATION OF INDEPENDENCE. HE WAS 33. AND ON JULY 4, 1776, THE FOUNDING FATHERS ADOPTED IT. A REVOLUTION WAS UNDER WAY.

A Declaration by the Representatives of the UNITED STATES

OF AMERICA, in General Congress assembled

When in the course of human events it becomes necessary for ~~a~~ people to
dissolve the political bands which have connected them with another, and to
~~assume among the~~ ~~that subordination which~~ ~~they have hitherto remained in &~~ as
one

assume among the powers of the earth the ~~equal~~ ~~separate & equal~~ station to
which the laws of nature & of nature's god entitle them, a decent respect
to the opinions of mankind requires that they should declare the causes
the
which impel them to ~~the change~~ separation.

We hold these truths to be ~~sacred & undeniable~~ that all men are
self-evident.
they are endowed by their creator with ~~equal~~
created equal ~~& independent;~~ that ~~from that equal creation they derive~~
rights ~~inherent & ~~inalienable, among ~~these~~ ~~which~~ are ~~the preservation of~~
inherent &
life, & liberty, & the pursuit of happiness; that to secure these ~~ends~~, ~~go~~
-vernments are instituted among men, deriving their just powers from
the consent of the governed; that whenever any form of government
shall becomes destructive of these ends, it is the right of the people to alter
or to abolish it, & to institute new government, laying it's foundation on
such principles & organising it's powers in such form, as to them shall
seem most likely to effect their safety & happiness. prudence indeed
will dictate that governments long established should not be changed for

HE WAS TALL and LEAN and SLEPT PARTLY SITTING UP in aN ALCOVE BED thAT divided his sTudy and DRESSING ROOM. HE woKE AT DAWN. I don't think he took NAPS.

HE sTudied HESSIAN FLIES and VOLTAIRE and MAPS of AFRICA and the KORAN and SHAKESPEARE. IN the Study were his tELESCOPES and PolygRaph Copying MAChiNE and RevolviNg BooK-STAND and BooKs. HE knew Greek, LatiN, FRench, SpaNish and ItALIAN. When he Read SpiNOZA, he READ him in LATIN. WHEN he Read EURiPidES, he READ him in GReeK. He wRote to AdAMs, "I CANNOT LivE Without BooKs." His Rooms were covered with PAINTINGs.

the Most important people were on the top.

He ReveRed thREE MEN: FRANCis BACON, of the JAUNTy TopPeR; ISAAC NEWTON, of the LuXURIouS LoCKs; and John LoCKE, of the LUXVRIoUS NOSE.

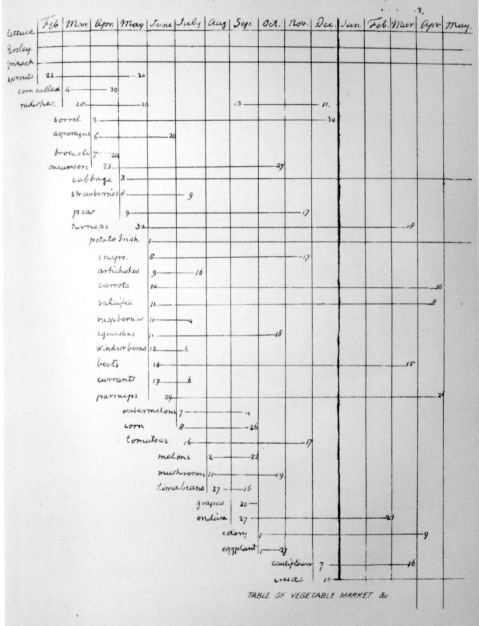

a Statement of the Vegetable market of Washington, during a period of 8 years, wherein the earliest & latest appearance of each article within the whole 8 years is noted.

37

	Feb.	Mar.	Apr.	May.	June	July	Aug	Sep.	Oct.	Nov.	Dec.	Jan.	Feb.	Mar.	Apr.	May.
lettuce																
Parsley.																
spinach																
sprouts	22			20												
corn sallad	4	30														
radishes.	20			31			13			11						
sorrel	3									30						
asparagus	6			26												
broccoli	7	24														
cucumbers	23							27								
cabbage	3															
strawberries	8			9												
peas	9							17								
turneps	30													18		
potato Irish	1															
snaps	5							17								
artichokes	9	16														
carrots	10														16	
salsify	11														8	
raspberries	11	4														
squashes	11						18									
Windsor beans	12	6														
beets	16													15		
currants	17	6														
parsneps	29														24	
watermelons		7				4										
corn		8			26											
tomatoes		16						17								
melons		2		22												
mushrooms		11					19									
lima beans		27	16													
grapes		20														
endive		27											29			
celery		1												9		
eggplant		1	27													
cauliflower		7											16			
cresses		16														

TABLE OF VEGETABLE MARKET &c

HE MADE CHARTS of EVERYTHING.
HIS FAVORITE VEGETABLE WAS PEAS.

IN PARIS, he WAS a WeLL-dRESSed MAN.

LATER, CLOTHES MATTERED LESS. His jACKET WAS
pATCHEd and SOCKS weRE SEWN into the LINING
FOR WARMTH.

HE WAS FRIENDS with JAMES (Little JIMMY) Madison
(who wROTE the CONSTITUTION, by the WAY), and DOLLEY
Madison, who was gRegARious and chARMing and
oFTEN SERVEd as JEFFERSON'S HostesS duRING his PRESidency.

DOLLEY lived long enough to be captured in a photograph wearing her dashing turban at the age of 80.

Among her last words were, "There is nothing in this world worth caring for."

The MARQUIS de LAFAYETTE, who HELPED FINANCE the AMERICAN REVOLUTION (and DID NOT get his HEAD chopped OFF DURING the FRENCH REVOLUTION) would come by and VISIT.

HE PROBABLY ate DOLLEY'S ICE CREAM.

JEFFERSON and he would STROLL in the GARDEN and PLUCK MaRSeiLLES Figs FROM the TREES. And while tHEY STROLLed and Ate the deLicious Figs, they would pass the slave quARters.

The MAN who wRote the DECLARation of Independence and said of SLaVeRy, "This ABOMINATION Must hAVE an END," WAS the OWNeR of SEVeRAL HUNDRED SLAVES. The MONUMeNtal Man hAD MONUMeNtaL FLAWS.

BARELY 30 years after his death
(on JULY 4, 1826), the CIVIL WAR EXPLODED.

And WHAT aBouT his relationship with
SALLY Hemings, one of his SLAVES?
It is Believed thAt she
gave birth to six of his children.

JefFeRson's father-in-law is thought
to have had a LiAison with the mother
of SALLy Hemings.
That would make SALLY and JeFFeRson's
wife, MARtha, haLF-sisters. AY cARamba!
And it was said that she Looked like
his beautiful, beloved, dead wife.
                    AY caRamba Again!

His friend, the Polish
Freedom Fighter TADEUSZ
Kosciuszko, LEFT MONEY
in his wiLL to be given
to JEFFERSON to FREE
and EDUCATE his SLAVES.
But the TASK WAS
overwhelming and he
DID NOT get it DONE.

Archaeologists are sifting through every grain of soil at Monticello to learn the story of what their lives were like – master and slaves.

Here is a Wedgwood creamware
fruit bowl they found.

Imagine the ELEGANT EVENINGS of brilliant discourse and fine WINE and the best of EVERYTHING. thomas playing the VIOLIN, Martha PLAYING the PIANOFORTE.

Alongside that, EVENINGS of ENDLESS LABOR and DEPRIVATION and FREEZING in PITIFULLY SMALL ROOMS, each one of which Housed an ENTIRE FAMILY. JEFFERSON WAS A KINDER MASTER than MOST. And he WAS greatly CONFLICTED.

136	1810. Dec.	linen	p?	cotton	blank	bed	hat	sifter	1810	linen	plain	cotton	blank	b
Burwell									Barnaby	7	3	2½	...	
Edwin		7	5½	.	. .		. .	1.	Lilly	7	2	3	..	
Joe		7	5½	.			.	1.	Anderson 6	2	..	1¾		1
Edy		homespun							Stannard 09	1	..	1		
James 05									John	7	3	2½	1	
Maria 07					.				Amy	7	2	3		
Davy		7	3	2½	..		.	1.	Ned	7	3	2½		
Fanny - - -									Jenny ...	7	2	3		
Ellen - 09									Aggy 98	4⅔	...	3¾		
Amy -									Israel 00	4	...	3¼		
Critta - - - -									Moses 03	3	...	2½		
Sally									Sucky 06	2	...	1¾		
Beverly - 98		4⅔	2	1¾					Molly	7	2	3		
Harriet 01		..	..	..					Bagwell ..	7	5½	.	.	
Madison 05									Minerva ..	7	2	3		
Eston - 08									Dec. 97	..	..	;	1.	
Betty Brown						1			Nanny 08	4	...	3¼		
Robert - 99		..	..	..					Willis 06	2	...	1¾	1	
Mary - 01		..	..	..					Archy 08	1⅓	...	1¼	1	
Peter Hemings		7	3	2½	1			.	Mary ...	7	2	3	1	
Nance						1								

It is a miserable part of the story, but it is not the whole story.

What else? He had terrible migraines and took to his bed for days at a time.

He gave excellent advice — to his daughter Patsy: "Determine never to be idle. No person will have occasion to complain of the WANT of TIME who NEVER LOSES ANY.

It is WONDERFUL HOW MUCH MAY BE DONE IF WE ARE ALWAYS DOING."

And to his friends:

"The object of walking is to Relax the Mind. You should therefore not permit yourself even to THINK while you WALK; but divert yourself by the OBJECTS surrounding you. WALKING is the BEST POSSIBLE EXERCISE."

I stood in his garden pavilion and imagined him
looking down the valley, or up at his house.
It is extraordinary that the building is still there.

WHEN JEFFERSON dIEd, in his 80s and
DEEPLY in DEBT, the FARM WAS Sold to
the LEVY FAMILY, who AdmiRed JeFFeRSon's
philosophy about SepaRation of church and State.
Jefferson Levy (I am suRe I went to his
BAR MiTzVah in the BRoNX, good old Jeff LEVy)
pReseRved it uNtiL 1923. Without the LEVYS,
Jefferson's Monticello world Not have SuRvived.

We stayed in a house NeaR Monticello that
had a stuNNiNg Room Jefferson designed foR
his fRiend. Now, thAt is a good FRiend.
(oveRleaf)

Here is Jeff (center) with his brothers,
Louis Napoleon and Mitchell Abraham.

History makes you HUNGRY.
We Ate CORNCAKES and gRiTs and
SAusages and EGGS and hAm Biscuits.
You NAMe iT.

Later, as we strolled back to the house, the littleleaf
lindens Released a pungent perfume. JEFFERSON's life WAS
epic, but a tiny moment captures the heart.

When Martha Jefferson lay dying at the age of 34,
after 10 years of marriage and giving birth to
six children, the desolate Thomas Jefferson
never left her side. They copied out their favorite
passage in the novel "Tristram Shandy."
First in her hand. Then in his.

time wastes too fast: every letter
I trace tells me with what rapidity
life follows my pen. the days and hours
of it are flying over our heads like
clouds of windy day. never to return —
more every thing presses on — and every
time I kiss thy hand to bid adieu, every absence which
follows it, are preludes to that eternal separation
which we are shortly to make!

JULY

★

Benjamin Franklin

Can Do

HE LOOKS A LITTLE HAUGHTY.
A TAD POMPOUS.
WELL, WHY NOT?

BENjAMIN FRANKLIN
WAS A
GENIUS,
ONE OF the 'GREAT
INVENTORS of
THIS COUNTRY.
WHAT did
HE do?
WELL,
EVERYTHING.

LET'S STRAIGHTEN OUT THE FIRST THING.
HE DIDN'T INVENT ELECTRICITY.

HE INVESTIGATED THE PRINCIPLES
OF ELECTRICITY AND INVENTED THE
LIGHTNING ROD.

AND, AMONG OTHER THINGS,
he INVENTED
BIFOCALS,
the CATHETER,
the
MECHANICAL
ARMONICA,
the
FRANKLIN
STOVE,

THE
ACTUAL
LIGHTNING ROD

SWIM
FINS
And

tHE ODOMETER.

HERE is the odometer thAT he GAVE To THomAS JEFFERSON.

HE BecAME WEALTHY FRoM his PRinting CompANY AND RETiReD AT The AGE of 42.

HE WAS the AuTHoR of
POOR RichArd's ALMANAC
AND gave SAGE AdviCE, Reaching
tEns of thousANds of pEoplE.

HE BELieVED iN DoinG GOOD.
EVERY DAY.

HE MADE chARTS AND had
DAILY GOALS

The morning question, What good shall I do this day?	5	Rise, wash, and address *Powerful Goodness;* contrive day's business and take the resolution of the day; prosecute the present study; and breakfast.
	6	
	7	
	8	
	9	Work.
	10	
	11	
	12	Read or overlook my accounts, and dine.
	1	
	2	Work.
	3	
	4	
	5	
	6	Put things in their places, supper, music, or diversion, or conversation; examination of the day.
	7	
	8	
	9	
Evening question, What good have I done today?	10	
	11	
	12	
	1	Sleep.
	2	
	3	
	4	

I don't think he WAS EVER BoREd.

HE SAW A dirty sTReeT and cReated
a SANiTaTioN depaRtment.

HE SAW A house ON FiRe and cReated
A FiRE DEPARTMENT.

HE SAW SicK PEOPLE and FouNded
a HOSpiTAL.

HE sTARted the FIRST
LENdiNG LiBRARy.

HE Saw people Needing an Education
and founded a UNiveRsity.

HE sTARTed the AMERiCAN PHiloJoPHiCAL
SociETy, whERE MEN and WOMEN
shaRed developments iN SciENCE.

And then, by the way,
he helped create and run the country.
He was a signer of both
the Declaration of Independence and the
Constitution.

He was Ambassador to France,
representing the fledgling United States.

BUT in THE MEANTIME, he HAD FUN.
TONS of FRENCH.
ARISTOCRATIC
FROU
FROU
FUN.

MARIE
ANTOINETTE
and the
WHOLE
GANG AT COURT
WERE NUTS
FOR him
with his
BRAINS and
his CRAZY
FUR
HAT.

And he FLIRTED with the WOMEN, who FLiRTed bACK.
HE WROTE THEM POEMS. THEY GAVE him GiFTS.

Madame Helvétius gave him this TEA SET.

BUT THE PARTY had to END. (WHY, I do NOT KNOW.)
And he RETURNED to AMERICA.
HE WOULD bECOME SO IMPORTANT To AMERICAN
IDENTITY THAT IN THE MidDLE of the 19th CENTURY

HERMAN MELVILLE WROTE A STORY WITH FRANKLIN IN IT.

BY then the WORLD WAS EXPLODING with INVENTIVENESS.
IN PARIS, in 1838, DAGUERRE WAS INVENTING PHOTOGRAPHY.

In 1845, in ENGLAND, the RUBBER BAND
MADE its APPEARANCE.

(DISCLOSURE: I AM a CO-FOUNDER of the
RUBBER BAND SOCIETY.)

AFTER the 1850's, thANKS in PART to FRANKLIN'S
iNFLUENCE, AMERICA bECAME the LANd of
iNGENUiTY. HeRe. in 1898, is NiKOLA TESLA, who
talKed to PigeoNS And woRKed with ElecTRiCiTy,
whiLE CALMly Reading A BooK.
I wish I KNew whAT he WAS READiNG.

THoMAS Edison WAS iNVENTiNG SoMeThiNG EVERY
FiVE MiNUTES. I BELiEVE he iNVENTEd the NAP.
HE couLdN'T TAKE OUT A PATENT oN ThAT,
though HE STiLL holds the RECORd FoR the
individUAL with the MOST PATeNTS.
AFTeR oNE of his NAPS, he iNVENTed the Light BulB.

AT A JELL-O Mold competition in BROOKLYN, RUN by this ENTERPRISING, BEAUTIFUL WOMAN IN A GREEN JACKET and YELLOW BLOUSE,

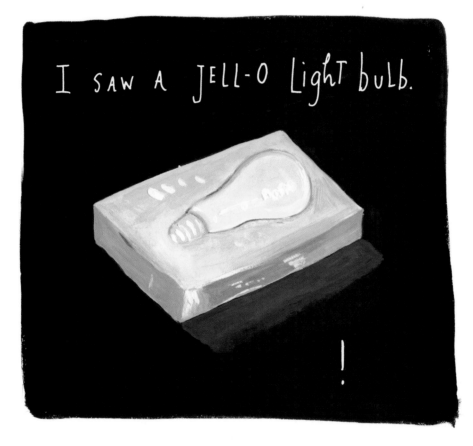

EVERYTHING IS INVENTED.
LANGUAGE. CHILDHOOD. CAREERS.
RELATIONSHIPS. RELIGION.
PHILOSOPHY. the FUTURE.
THEY ARE NOT THERE FOR the PLUCKING.
THEY DON'T EXIST IN SOME
    NATURAL STATE.
THEY MUST BE INVENTED BY PEOPLE.
AND thAT, OF COURSE, IS A GREAT THING.

DON'T MOPE in YOUR ROOM.
GO INVENT SOMETHING.
THAT IS the AMERICAN MESSAGE.

ELECTRICITY. FLIGHT. The TELEPHONE.
TELEVISION. COMPUTERS. WALKING ON
the MOON. IT NEVER STOPS.

SOME THINGS HAVE ALReadY BEEN INVENted.
AND WE ARE VERY GRATEFUL.
IN the PIN DEPARTMENT:
    The SAFETY PIN.

W. Hunt.
Pin.

Nº 6281.   Patented Apr. 10. 1849.

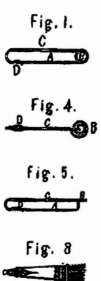

Fig. 1.

Fig. 2.

Fig. 4.

Fig. 3.

Fig. 5.

Fig. 6.

Fig. 8.

Fig. 7.

The indispensable Bobby Pin.

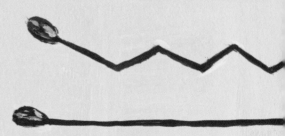

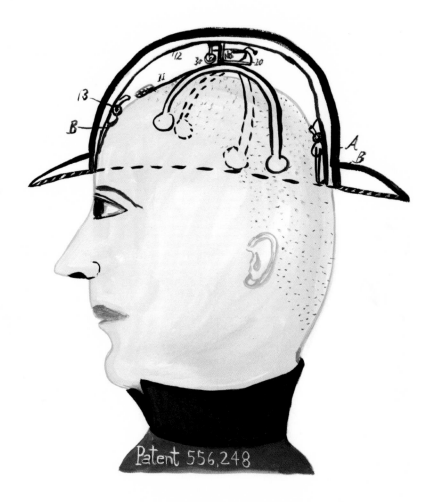

In the ETIQUETTE DEPARTMENT:

The self-tipping HAT FOR the MAN

who hAs pACKAges in his HANds.

In the PATENT OFFICE in ALEXANDRIA, VA., thousands of PATENT EXAMINERS STUDY EVERY COCKAMAMIE GIZMO and BRILLIANT INNOVATION and LIFE-SAVING DEVICE.
IF you GET A PATENT, it LASTS FOR 20 YEARS and thAT is that. UNLESS you GET a TRADEMARK and WRANGLE TRADE-SECRET STATUS, like COCA-COLA with its SECRET INGREDIENT 7X!
By the WAY,
you can PATENT a PEACH.

which BRINGS ME to A LUNCH with
a BeaUTIFUL GREEN-EYED MAN NAMED FRITZ,
who LOOKS EXACTLY LIKE

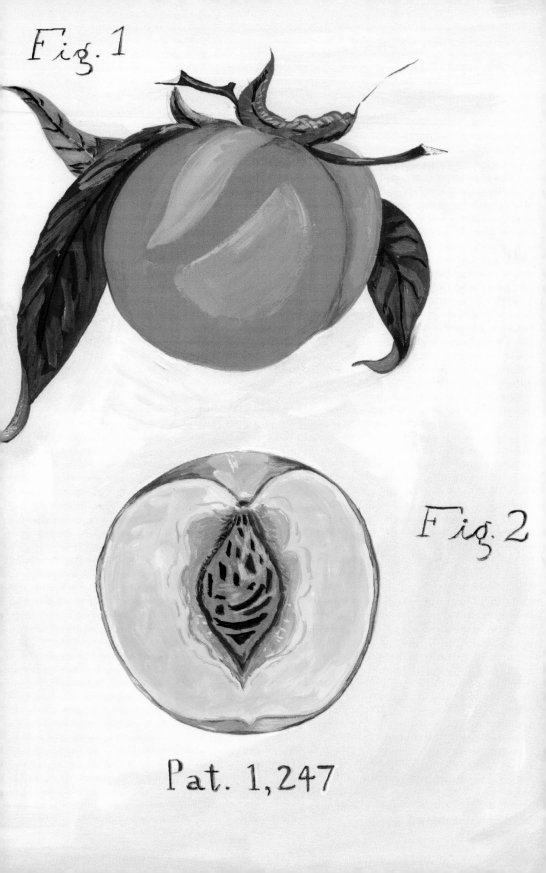

Fig. 1

Fig. 2

Pat. 1,247

HERMAN MELVILLE. OVER A FRIED EGG, FRITZ TOLD ME ABOUT THE BOTANIST JOHN BARTRAM. BARTRAM WAS A GREAT FRIEND OF FRANKLIN

and Named a SENSUAL, NOT POMPOUS
CAMELLIA-LiKE tree in his HONOR,

the
FRANKLiNiA,
which BLOOMS
LUSCiOUSLY
in
LATe SUMMeR.

And I am NOT INVENTING ANY of this.

AUGUST

★

James Buchanan

WHAT ARE WE DOING HERE?
Who KNOWS?
How did WE GET HERE?
I'LL tell YOU.

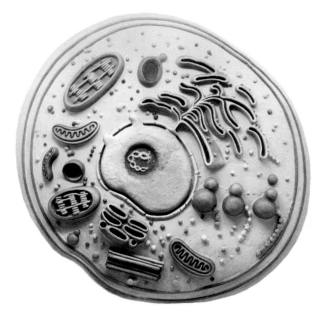

FIRST there WAS A PRIMORDIAL SOUP,
teeming with PLAY-Doh- LIKE BLOOKIES.

THESE EVOLVED INTO

Soignée Diatoms.

Growing tired of the OCEAN, CREATURES MiGRated onto the LAND.

THEN CAME DiNoSAURS and MotoRcycleS.

PEOPLE! WALKed (SLOWLY, SLOWLY) ACROSS the
LAND BRidge KNOWN as BERiNgiA (EATiNG HERRiNgiA?)
CONNECTiNG ASiA to this CONTiNENT.

CiViLiZATiONS FLOURiShED.

LANGUAGE. MUSiC. ART. AGRiCULTURE. RiTUAL. LAW.
The CLANS EvoLved iNTo the 500 NATiVE AMERiCAN TRiBES
THAT STiLL EXiST ToDAY.
THEy hAd BeautiFUL NAMES thAT I am SEWiNG oN FABRiC.

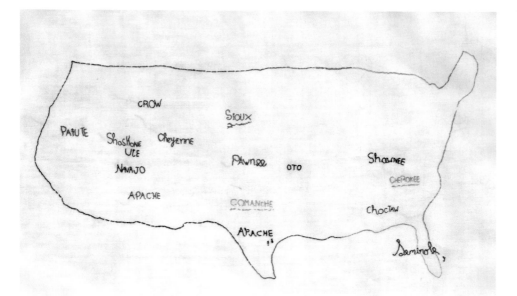

BY 1100 A.D., the NORSE, Led by
LEiF ERiCSON,
TooK to the SEA, REAChiNG NEWFouNdLand,

WHERE THEY RAPED,
PILLAGED
and
GENERALLY
WREAKED
HAVOC.
DECIDING
THERE WAS
NO PLACE
LIKE HOME,
THEY Returned
to NORTHERN
EUROPE
without telling
ANYONE WHERE
THEY HAD
BEEN.

So the WESTERN HEMISPHERE WAS pRetty MUCH
A SECRET to the EUROPEANS UNTiL

COLUMBUS,
LOOKING
FOR A
ShoRT CuT
to
INDIA,
CAME
SAILING
IN.

The SPANISH ARRIVED in FORCE.
PONCE de LEÓN CAME.

THEN de SOTO CRUISED IN,

ON his SNAPPY RED
DESoTo.

The SPANIARDS BROUGHT MORE than CARS.
THEY BROUGHT diSEASE and BRUTALITY. It did NOT
TAKE LONG FOR the NATIVE AMERICAN POPULATION
To DROP FROM 10 MILLION to 500,000.

BY THAT time PEOPLe BEGAN to hAVE AN IDEA
OF WHAT the WORLd LOOKEd LiKE.
SEBASTIAN MÜNSTER'S MAP had a FEW TINY INACCURACIES.

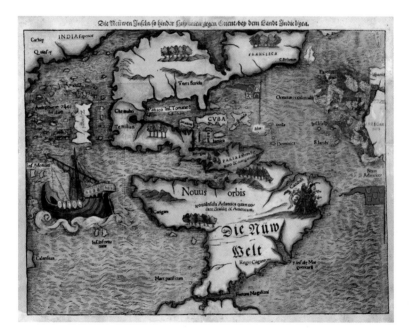

FOUR HUNDRed YEARS AGO HENRY HUDSON
SAiLEd IN WEARING RUFFLES, which FORTUNATELY
DID NOT CATCH ON in thE
NEW WORLd.

IN OUR FAMILY WE had VERY
WARM FeeLings ABOUT HENRY HUDSON.
NOT ONLY did WE LiVE at 2675 HENRY
HUDSON PARKWAY,

but the PARK WHERE I would sit in a
tree READING for hours WAS called
HENRY   HUDSON
                    PARK.

THEN CAME COMMERCE and GReed. MiLLioNS oF PEoPLE
KidNapped fRom AFRiCA, tHROWN into a LiViNG HELL
and BRought HERe to BE SLAVES.
WELCOME to youR NEW HoME.
THeN, the AMERiCAN REvoLutioN. MANiFEST DEStiNY.
LAND GRABBiNg. The INdusTRiAL REvoLutioN.
The BRookLYN BRidgE. ANd, oF CouRSE,
CoNEY ISLAND
with its BARREL oF LoVE RidE,
which SiGMUNd FREUd SuReLY ENjoYed
duRiNg his SoLE TRip to AMERiCA in 1909.

(perhaps after EATING A
SLIGHTLY STALE
CUPCAKE),

MASSES OF HUMANITY KEPT POURING IN.
GERMANS. RUSSIANS. ITALIANS. IRISH.
THEY SAILED INTO NEW YORK HARBOR,
    PAST THE SPLENDID SYMBOL OF FREEDOM.

    THEY ARRIVED AT ELLIS ISLAND.
IN THE MAJESTIC ROOMS OF THE MAIN BUILDING
THOUSANDS OF PEOPLE WERE INSPECTED, EXAMINED,
TAGGED AND SORTED. MOST MADE IT IN. SOME WERE SENT BACK.
I LOOK AT THE PHOTOGRAPH OF THESE TWO GIRLS,
    AND THINK THEY COULD HAVE BEEN MY SISTER AND ME.
BUT WE CAME HERE IN 1954 AND FLEW IN ON A LUMBERING
JET WITH MY FATHER, WHO WAS SMOKING A CIGARETTE ON
THE PLANE, PLAYING GIN RUMMY AND DRINKING SCOTCH.
WE MOVED TO RIVERDALE, WHERE MY MOTHER WOULD NOT
LET ME JOIN THE GIRL SCOUTS BECAUSE SHE DID NOT WANT
ME TO LOSE MY ISRAELI IDENTITY. AND NOW?
STILL, HUNDREDS OF THOUSANDS OF PEOPLE WANT TO BECOME AMERICANS.
    WHAT IS IT ABOUT THIS PLACE?

I visit Andrea Quarantillo, who works for the Department of Homeland Security.

She is the district director for citizenship and immigration. Her family came here from Sicily in 1906.

I expect her to be intimidating and officious (it is Homeland Security, after all) but she is human and warm and welcoming.

She speaks at the small swearing-in ceremony that I attend. When I became a citizen, an official told us we would shed our old identity and put on a new identity - "Like taking off an old sweater and putting on a new one." Andrea says the opposite: This Nation's identity is based on its rich diversity. Immigrants are becoming Americans, and an American can be many different things.

Every year close to one million people become citizens. A rather startling statistic. At the swearing-in ceremony, I meet Bolivar Napoleon Mendez from Bolivia. A woman from Saudi Arabia. A man from Mali.

We Meet a Man FROM ECUADOR who
Reminds me of my UNCLE SHLOMO,

And Murray Richter, who works for immigration,
whose mother NETTIE came to America from
Russia and opened a fruit stand on Dumont
Avenue in BROOKLYN.

This is a completely NEW AMERICA, more
culturally complex than anyone could have
imagined. And the QUESTION keeps coming up,
"WHOSE HOME is this?"

WHAT of the 12 MILLION PEOPLE living here who
are undocumented?
THEY are here illegally. Do they deserve to stay?
There are groups lobbying for immigration reform.
At community centers you meet dedicated organizers
and undocumented people, and you think these are
GREAT people and they cannot be sent back to
their countries of origin. The problems
are SUBSTANTIAL: Health care. Employment. Taxes.
Detention facilities. Impenetrable bureaucracies.
Is it Naïve of me to think, while acknowledging
the myriad problems, that the system is basically just?

And then.
In Queens
we enjoy a
MANGO
LASSi
at the
JACKSON
DINER.

THEN WE STROLL through an INDIAN
SUPERMARKET and buy

A BOX of COOKIES FROM PAKISTAN.

"THINK SMALL" IS MY NEW MOTTO.
IT HELPS ME HANDLE the COMPLICATED
TOO-MUCHNESS OF IT ALL.

WE POP OVER to the BRONX to UNITED PICKLE
to SAY hELLO to STEVE LEIBOWITZ, the OWNER,
and his EMPLOYEES VISHNUDAT LOOTAWAN and
JOSÉ TORRES JR., whoSE fAThER WAS A GREAT
BOXER and WRITER. WE LEAVE, PASSING
SCHMUGER'S HARDWARE,
   which is NOT fAR fRom the BUcOLic
WOODLAWN CEMeTERY, whERe the diminutive
immigrant IRVING BERLIN is buRied.

IF BERLIN hAd Not been allowed to come to this
COUNTRY, WE WOULd NEVER HAVE had the
SUBLIME PLEASURe of SEEING FRED daNCE
with GingeR while SeReNading heR with
BERLIN'S LYRICS

"HEAVEN, I'M iN HEAVEN,
AND my HEARt BEATS So
that I caN HARdly
SPEAK,
and I SEEM to
FiNd the
HAPPINESS
I Seek,
wheN WE'Re
out TogetHeR
DANCiNg
cheek
to
cheek."

SEPTEMBER

★

Dolley Madison

For Goodness' Sake

I
HAD
The
DREAM
AGAIN.

I AM STANDING IN A SPOTLESS ROOM with the COMMISSIONER of SANiTATioN.

THERE is COMPLETE HARMONY beTWEEN US. WE do NoT NEEd to SAY A WORD.

HE IS WEARING
A GRAY suit with the
USUAL ORANGE
fouLArd.

RIDICULOUS, YOU SAY?
  NOT SO RIDICULOUS.
MY LOVE of NEW YORK CITY and
   LOVE oF CLEANING ARE
      WELL KNOWN.
   A CLEAN CITY IS A BEAUTIFUL CITY.
   And I want to HELP.

MY CITY IS LIKE ANY CITY:
MIND-BOGGLINGLY COMPLEX.
MORE than 300,000 pEople aRE
  in PUBLIC SERVICE.
    And the MAYOR is thE
        BOSS.
I go to visit his office in
       CITY HALL.
  On the WAY I SEE thE USUAL.

PEOPLE
RUNNING
HeRe and THERE.

peopLE playing Chess.

PEOPLE BEING
DESPONDENT.

Nathan Hale stands outside.

He was executed
by the British
when he was
only 21. I
am so sad for
Nathan and his Mother.

NATHAN HALE

I ONLY
REGRET THAT
·HAVE BUT
ONE LIFE TO
LOSE FOR MY
COUNTRY.

The building is
Elegant.
Lincoln Lay in
STATE
HERE.

We have George Washington's desk.

The CENTER of ACTION is the GIANT ROOM where the MAYOR and his STAFF WORK. No Closed DOORS FOR this MAYOR. HE sits in the CENTER of A PARK of DESKS. HE is USUALLY there at 7:30 A.M.

I had expected people to be running around with their hair on fire, but it is unexpectedly tranquil. Where are the miserable public servants in gloomy offices? Where is Bartleby the Scrivener? The staff is young and good-looking, positive and hard-working.

I meet HAEDA MihaltSES, the diRector of the Office of InterGovernmental AFFAIRS.

I MEEt John RhEA,
head of the New York City
          Housing Authority.
The daunting job of
          creating affoRdable
Housing foR HundReds of
thousAnds of people fALLs
on his shoulders. HE
is woRKing with MEGAN SHEEKEY,
   pResident of the MAYOR'S
   Fund to Advance the
   City of New YORK.

          I love thAt
          Fund.

I FIND OUT ABOUT the CITY'S
MONUMENTAL NEW SERVICE
INITIATIVE. ARE WE
READY To VOLUNTEER and
Find MEANINGFUL, UNCYNICAL
INVOLVEMENT in OUR COMMUNITIES?
WE MIGHT BE.

I LEAVE the BuildiNG and RUN
SMACK into ANOTHER PART of
CITY BUSINESS, the
MARRIAGE BUREAU.

The Rooms are FANCIER thAN thEY have EVER BEEN, but the FLIMSY ticket is disAppointing.

We CouLd do BETTER. It is MaRRiage, afTeR ALL.

Office of the City Clerk
The City of New York

C617

Please have a
seat in the Ceremony
waiting area.

3:10pm   9.07.09

And AFTeR the WEddiNg (You CAN BRing UP To 30 PEOPLE with you), how ABOUT a NICE LUNch at EXCELLeNt DUMPLiNG?

YES indeed.

GoodbYE, CRAZY EXPENSiVE, GiANt WEDDiNGS.

But BACK to GARBAGE, and WHILe we are at it,
its GLOPPY TWIN, SEWAGE.

I speak to Vito Turso, a deputy Commissioner of
SANitation, and he Explains the trip my

packet of old love letters, thrown away
in a rash moment, takes.

Every DAY Nearly 8,000 of
New York's Strongest pick up
12,000 Tons of Garbage and
RECYCLABLes.

Garbage is sent to Big pits, called
"Tipping Floors", at WASTE Transfer
STATIONS. BULLdozers push the
garbage onto Conveyor Belts.
It is then Compacted and put
into MASSIVE Shipping containers.
The containers are placed on
FLATBed Rail Cars pulled by
Locomotives. And VoiLA!
Au Revoir, garbage.

MANHATTAN REFUSE goes to a
WASTE-to-ENERGY plant in
ESSEX, N.J.

BRONX, BROOKLYN and QUEENS
REFUSE is SENT by RAIL OR TRUCKS
to PENNSYLVANIA OR OHIO landfills.

STATEN ISLAND REFUSE goES to my
PERSONAL FAVORITE, South CAROLINA.

And the SEWAGE?

Ah, the SEWAGE.

The 53-ACRE NEWTOWN CReek
SewAge PLANT in
GReenpoint, BRooklyN,
is A ReVELATioN.

I Go there EARLY ONE MORNING.
OH MAMA.

CHRISTINE HOLOWACZ IS WATERING THE LITTLE GARDEN in FRONT of the VISITOR CENTER.

she WORKS with the city to ADDRESS the Needs and CONCERNS of the community. INSIDE the visitor CENTER is an ART INSTALLATION by VITO ACCONCI.

JAMES PYNN is the PLANT SUPERVISOR.

HE gives US A TOUR of the STUPENDOUS
DIGESTER EGGS - the heart of the COMPLEX.

THEY WERE designED by PolsHEK PARTnership ARCHitects.

The things we lEARN about couLd moRe than
FilL a digester EGG: SLUDGE, MUCK, MiLLioNS
OF PoUNDS OF GooPY LiQUiDS, BoilERS, AERATioN
TANKS, PHLANGES, SPRoCKETS, CARBoN BEDS,
MASSiVE FiLTERS, MoNSTeR PiPES, EFFLUENT
THiNGS, CENTRiFUGES and oF CoURSE

the UTTERLY Adorable Condensation Pot.

WE GO to thE TOP of the EGGS
and WALK aloNG the UTiLiDOR.

SuFFICE iT TO SAY, You would be
veRy HAppy to get MaRRied up HERE.

And there is NO smell.

WHAT?

After dark, the plaNt Looks like something
out oF "The ARABiAN NiGHTS" thanks
to the Lighting dESigNed by
L'OBSeRVAToiRe INteRNATioNAL.

After visiting the PLANT, WE GO ON the creekside Nature WALK, designed by GEORGE TRAKAS.

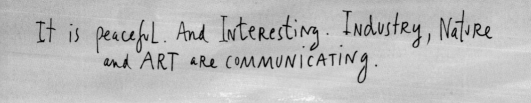

It is peaceful. And Interesting. Industry, Nature and ART are COMMUNICATING.

A city CAN BE OPTIMISTIC.
Now I Need to decide whAT iT is
thAT I will voluNteeR FoR .
IT will hAVE Something to do with
making the CiTY SpARKLing and
SHINING.

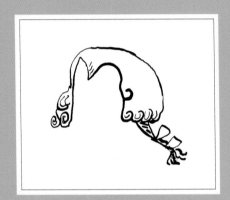

OCTOBER

★

James Madison

WE HOPE. WE DESPAIR.
WE hope. WE dESpAIR.
THAT is whAT GOVERNS US.
WE hAVE a BipoLAR SYSTEM.

ARMEd with this KnowLedge,

A PHOTO OF A WOMAN DANCING

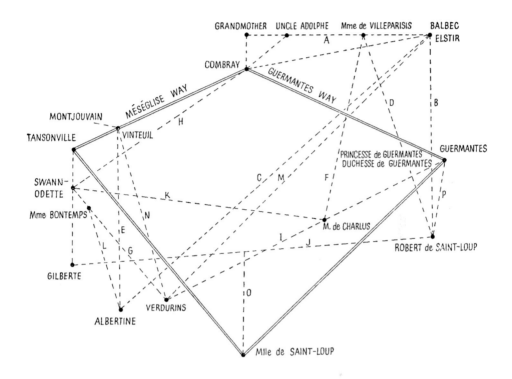

GRANDMOTHER   UNCLE ADOLPHE   Mme de VILLEPARISIS   BALBEC
A   ELSTIR

COMBRAY
GUERMANTES WAY
B

MÉSÉGLISE WAY
D

MONTJOUVAIN
H

TANSONVILLE   VINTEUIL

PRINCESSE de GUERMANTES   GUERMANTES
DUCHESSE de GUERMANTES

SWANN-   C   M   F   P
ODETTE   K

Mme BONTEMPS   N

E   M. de CHARLUS

L   G   I   J   ROBERT de SAINT-LOUP

GILBERTE

O

VERDURINS

ALBERTINE   Mlle de SAINT-LOUP

and an indispensable chart of
Marcel Proust's work,

I visit our nation's capital

and the CAPITOL BUILDING.

Before 9/11 you could
Go in and wander around
La-di-da.
But now, forget about it.

It is a STATELY and GRaNd Edifice. FuLL of
STatues, tassels, cAthedRaL DOMES and MaRBle.

The ARched coRRidoRS aRE decoRAted with LAvish fRescoes
cREAted in thE 1800s bY ConstantiNo BRumidi, aN
ARTist who had WoRKed in thE VATICAN beFoRE
hE imMigRated to AMERICA.

Good cRedentiaLS.

ROMAN
GODDESS OF WAR

APPROPRIATIONS.

But don't be seduced by the grandeur.
The MESSAGE HERE is LiBERTy and EQUALiTY.
THERe are QuotATiONS everywhere.
Above the MEN'S ROOM.

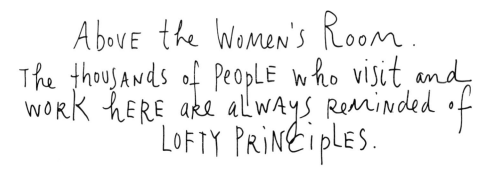

Above the Women's Room.
The thousands of people who visit and work here are always reminded of LOFTY PRINCIPLES.

(The bathrooms are bipartisan.)

The FLOORS are polished to the point of Ecstasy.
And surprisingly, dogs are welcome to accompany politicians.
Both Democratic and Republican dogs.

(The FLOORS are bipartisan.)

And they wait patiently as OFFICIALS have meetings.

The fresh-faced, super-polite teenage pages run around helping the officials.

THE ELEVATOR OPERATORS ARE SPIFFY.

THE UNDERGROUND TRAM CONDUCTOR SPORTS A DASHING CAP.

AND THERE ARE TREASURES IN THE BASEMENT, LIKE A
MASSIVE MARBLE BATHTUB USED BY OFFICIALS
BACK IN THE DAY.

BUT WHAT is EVERYONE doing HERE?

WE have a Bicameral Legislature.
That's the beauty of American Democracy.

The SENATE has 100 Senators and
the House of Representatives has
435 representatives.

SENATORS SERVE SIX-YEAR TERMS.

REPRESENTATIVES SERVE Two-Year TERMS.

RIGHT AWAY you CAN see PROBLEMS
with that SETUP.

WHEN a LAW is pROpoSEd, the House and the SENATe cREATe theiR owN SEPARATE BiLLS AT The SAME TIME.

OH-OH.

THEN, thRough A SERIES OF INSANELY COMPLICATEd MACHiNations that INCLVDE COMMiTTEES, SUBCOMMiTTEES, HEARINGS, CAUCUSES, CONFERENCES, QVORVMS, FiLiBusteRS, LOBBYiNG, EARMARKS ANd UNBeLievABLE COMPROMISES, the BiLLS MUSt be WRitteN, voted oN and pASSed.

THEN (bEFORE YOU GET TOO HAPPY),
the HOUSE and SENATE MUST RECONCILE
tHEIR BILLS (don't ASK) and SEND
ONE FINAL BILL to the PRESIDENT
to BE SIGNed iNto LAW.
(My BRAiN is bifuRCAtiNg just
thinKing about it.)
The system is SUPPOSEd to be CUMbERSOME.
Not subjEct to the whim of the MoMeNt.

And then you think about the people
who do this woRK and wondeR,
ARE tHEY CRAZY PEOplE?

WELL, SoMe, YES!

But you meet otHeRS and think,
thEy aRE SMARt and good pEOplE.

I meet:
Rosa DeLauro,
a democratic
Representative from
Connecticut.

JACK REED,
A DEMOCRATIC SENATOR
FROM
Rhode Island.

I watch Senator Max Baucus of
empty Senate chamber talking

Montana stand in the
about his health care bill.

I watch an incomprehensible
House subcommittee meeting on derivatives
led by the feisty Barney Frank
of Massachusetts, where Experts
use the word "Transparency"
20 times in one hour.

I watch Senate Floor votes
on I don't know what —
with Orrin Hatch of Utah
and
John McCain of Arizona
and Al Franken of Minnesota
and Olympia Snowe of Maine,
who are ALL standing
around chatting and having
A convivial time.

THEY WORK INCREDIBLY HARD.

THEY have to RAISE MONEY (BIG PROBLEMS hERE)
and MaKE MaNY pROMISES, MANY OF which
they CANNot Keep.

THEY have to COURT VOTES.

How CAN pEOPLE do ALL of thAT and
MAINTAIN INTEGRITY?
THEY must have STAMINA.
They must be OPTIMISTIC!

THEY NEED to UNderStANd Mountains
of INFORMATION.
FOR this theY RELY on their STAFF.

I meet Luke Swarthout,
a young staffer for Senator
Tom Harkin of Iowa. His
intelligence and humility make me
believe in our future.

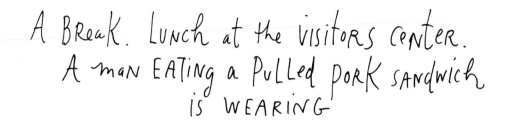

A BREAK. LUNCH at the VISITORS CENTER.
A MAN EATING a PuLLed poRK SANdwich
IS WEARING

A PORKPIE HAT.

I go to the AMERICAN BOUNTY counter and order a TURKEY PLATTER.

THANKsgiving is NOT fAR away, and I am feeLing thankful.
CoNFUSed. But thANKFuL.

At night I go to a museum to look
at MODERN art and SEE PEOPLE who
are DEFINITELY NOT iN PoLitics.
I Realize that being in the CAPiTAL is
like being in A TIME MACHINE.

Even though ALL the work is ABOUT CREATING LAWS foR the FuTuRE, CoNgRess's mANdate is bAsed on the CoNstitutioN and the philosophy of the founders. THEIR PRESENCE IS FelT AT EVERY TuRN.

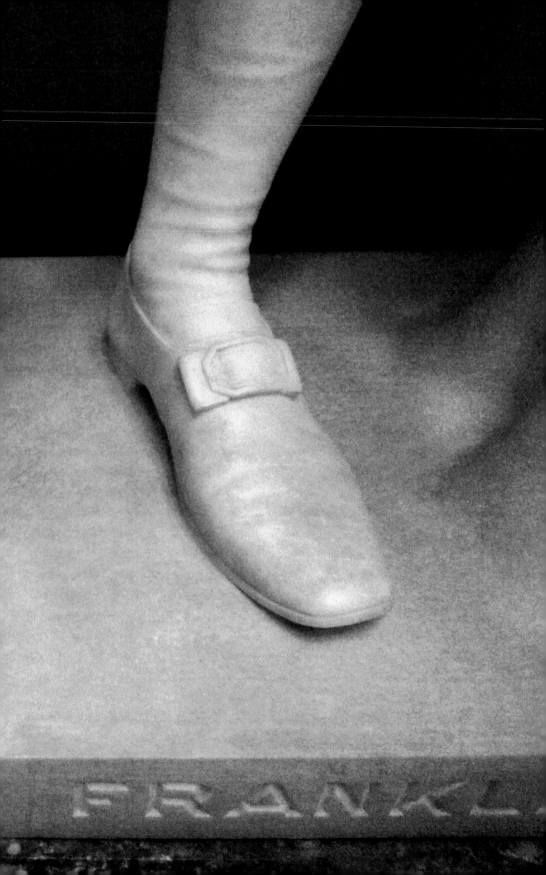

And what will happen now?
Bills will be passed into LAW.
And if they are not perfect
Don't DESPAIR.
There is Hope that the
system could work
and they can be
MENDED.
AMENDED.
AMEN.

Annuit Coeptis
providence has favored our undertaking

Novus Ordo Seclorum
A new order of the Ages

E Pluribus Unum
out of Many, one

NOVEMBER

★

James Monroe

THANKSGIVING.
SINCE the BEGINNING, AMERICANS
have CONNECTed the BOUNTY
of the LANd and
the GOODNESS of LiFE
to DEMOCRACY.

WAShington, ADAMS,
JEFFERSON, MADISON—
fARMeRS ALL— enVISioNed
an AGRARiAN SociETy.
WE have SINCE EVoLVed into
a VERY diffeRent Kind of Society.

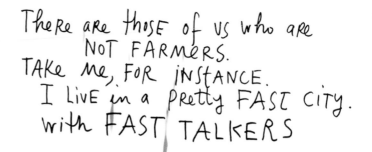

There are those of us who are NOT FARMERS.
TAKE me, FOR INSTANCE.
I LiVE in a pretty FAST CiTY.
with FAST TALKERS

and FAST WALKERS.

And WE
have
FAST FOOD.

EVERY
CITY
DOES.

And EVERY SUBURB. And EVERY

LittLE Bit of this couNtRy hAs

VERY FAST FOOD.
IF YOU EAT TOO MUCH of THIS FOOD,
YOU BECOME SICK and ALSO FATAFAT.
AND NO AMOUNT OF FATAFAT
PILLS WILL HELP YOU.

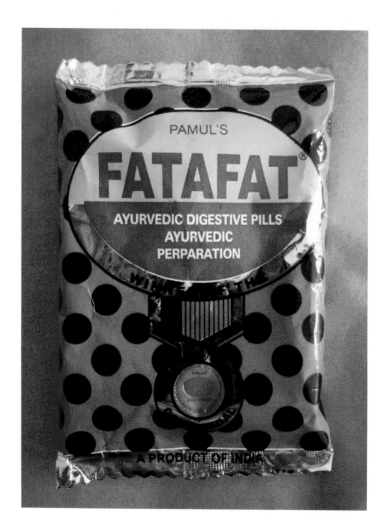

You would Need to WALK to CALIFORNIA
to WORK off the EXCESS. WhiCh is WhAT I did.

IN my hEAd.

Flying in the CATASTROPHIC
  CARBON-IMPRINT VEHICLE,
 EATING the CATASTROPHIC AIRPLANE FooD,
I LooKed at the CoUNTRY.

Things LooK clear-and NATuRALLY
 AgRARiaN-FRom this HEight.

I SEE SHEEP. I see LittlE Bo PEEP.

But thAT is NoT The WAY iT
     REALLY is.

Is thERE SoME INHERENT VALUE
  To thAT WAY oF LiFE ThAT
      WE hAVE LoST?

Is thERE SoME EleMeNT oF DEMocRACY
   thAt is DiMiNishEd?

  WE CAN'T ALL Be FARMeRS.
  You would NoT want to RELy on ME
    FoR YouR FooD.
 And whAT ABouT GETTiNG the
     GooD FooD?

Do the WEALThy hAVE ACCESS to the
 ReAlly hEALthy FooD whiLE the
  Less AFFLueNt do NoT?

WHEN you LooK at it that WAY,
it DOES NOT feeL AT aLL liKe
a DEMocRACy.
The FABRic of ouR LiVES is Bound
in the Food thAt WE EAT and
the WAY we Sit down to eAt.
WHAT is GoiNG oN NoW?

ALiCE WATERS has inviTEd mE
to visit hER PROGRAM CALLed
The EdiBLE SCHooLyARd,
to see the woRK bEINg doNE in
CALiFoRNiA.

CALiFoRNiA.
LANd of iMMENSE and ANcieNT
tREES CoveREd in LichEN.

Land of cows that we eat.
Should we? Shouldn't we?

I GO to HER RESTAURANT CHEZ PANISSE AND SIT AT A TABLE in the KITCHEN.

The Food is Bought FROM LOCAL ORGANIC FARMERS. JEROME, who is A CHEF and an ARTIST, tells me ABOUT

F.T. MARINETTI'S "FUTURIST COOKBOOK." MARINETTI CAME UP with conceptUAL PROJECTS FOR DINING.

The wearing of sponge
PAJAMAS. The eating
of COD LIVER OIL. Hmmm.

The comings and goings of this Restaurant kitchen warm my heart.

I visit BOB CANNARD's FARM.

HE DOES NOT SPRAY his CROPS. HE BELIEVES THERE is NO
such thing AS A BAD BUG. (HE LOVES ALL BUGS!)
A plant WILL PROTECT iTSeLF NATURALLY if it is HEALthy.
I AM SURE GEORGE WAShiNGTON would have WANTED to
TALK To him. And Thomas JeFFeRSON as WELL.
   WE SiT DOWN TO LUNCh.

It is simple and BEAUTIFUL.

I LOOK at the CARROTS in his SINK.

BOB tELLS ME thAT thESE ORgaNic CARROTS CONTAIN MORE NUTRIENTS ThAN CARROTS NOT GROWN ORGANICALLY. So WHAT DO WE dO ABOUT ThAT?

I MEET MICHAEL POLLAN, the AUTHOR of "THE OMNIVORE'S DILEMMA,"
FOR A WALK. OF COURSE, he FINDS MUSHROOMS.

THEY HAVE SPRUNG UP OVERNIGHT AND he SPOTS THEM in
the PINE NEEDLES. HIS WORDS HAVE BECOME AN INTERNATIONAL
MANTRA: "EAT FOOD. NOT TOO MUCH. MOSTLY PLANTS."

HE INTERVIEWS WENDELL BERRY, A WRITER and FARMER
who is so connected to the LAND that he USES A
HORSE-DRAWN PLOW.

I visit the EDiBLE Schoolyard of the MARTIN LUTHER
KiNG JR. MiDDLE School in BERKELEY.

The chilDREN work in a huge VEgetablE and FRUit
garden where chickENS wandeR about HAPPiLY.

The chilDREN Sow and REAP. They pick beans and KalE
and pineapple guAVAS. They RoAst PEPPeRS.

They CHURN BUTTeR. AND They CooK.

And then they sit down together and EAT.
And TALK. And PHILOSOPHIZE.

Which is more powerful:
love or hate?

Asked whether they are OPTIMISTS or PESSIMISTS, THESE
Boys said they are "PESSIMISTS,

BUT HAPPY ONES!"

And then they fold the TABLECLOTH. And SWEEP. And do ALL the things that FAMILIES have Been Doing for Hundreds of YEARS.

Except MANY children often Do NOT sit DOWN to MEALS with their own FAMILIES. And SOME drink SODA for BREAKFAST. So what Do WE do About that?

I MEET MICKEY Murch and his FAMILY on their FARM. Mickey has BUILT A COCKAMAMIE CONTRAPTION

To RIDE into TOWN where he COOKS FRESH Food. this is my Kind of CONTRAPTION.

Now I am getting FLASHBACKS to the '60s.
        But it is different.
It is NOT dropping out (though that sounds
        tempting Now and thEN).
It is bringing ELemental things to
        the PRESENT time with COMMERCE
                and opTIMISM.
CAN that work? CAN giANT AGRIBUSINESS
SHRINK, while TRUE ORGANIC FARMS GROW?
    CAN the ELITISM of A FARMeRS' MARKeT SHIFT so
THAT the ORGANIC FARMS CAN BE SUBSIDIZed and thAT

PRICES ARE REASONABLE FOR ALL PEOPLE? ThAT would BE
A DEMOCRACY OF HEALThy EATING.
    I Go To ALICE'S HOUSE and She COOKS an EGG.
    WHeN ALICE COOKS AN Egg it is No ORDINARY EVENT.

SHe USES A LARGE SPOON madE by her friend Angelo Garro, an ARTIST BLACKSMITH.

THE EGG fROM the ARAUCANA chickEN GOES onto the SPOON thAT gets hEld im the FIRE foR a FEW miNUTES.

And thEN the EGG is put on toAst and eATEN with TREmendovs JOY.

HuRRah FoR the chicken.

HuRRah FoR the EGG.

EARLY ONE MORNING I go FOR A WALK.
I SEE A WOMAN WHO I KNOW IS A BIT OUT
  OF HER MIND. I LIKE HER.
SHE IS WALKING IN A KIND OF TRANCE,
GOING FROM TREE TO TREE, STOPPING

AT each ONE
TO LOOK UP AT
the LEAVES.

IS SHE ACTING this WAY BECAUSE SHE DRANK
SODA FOR Breakfast HER WHOLE LIFE?

ONCE AGAIN, I WALK ACROSS
the COUNTRY.

IN MY hEAd.

I visit another school that will have an
EDIBLE Schoolyard. This will be the first one in
NEW YORK CITY. At the ARTURO TOSCANINI Elementary
School on Avenue X in Brooklyn.
CELIA KAPLINSKY, the captivating Principal, tells me
what CICERO said: "If you have a garden and A
LIBRARY, you have EVERYTHING you NEED."
THERE will BE A VEGETABLE and Fruit garden wHERE A
PARKING lot is Now. The children will work
and cook and take that EXPERIENCE to their FAMILIES.

And there will be bounty of a
different kind in this country.

THE United States of America
could be less FASTLY FASTLY
and MORE SLOWLY SLOWLY. WE could
think SMALL and shift to A NEW (old)
WAy of growing food and EATing and
BEing. Something that would make
the FounDERS HAPPY.

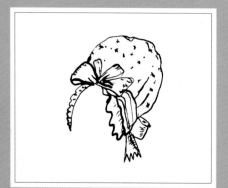

DECEMBER

★

Martha Washington

By George

GEORGE.

GEORGE.
HE IS
EVERYWHERE.

on A TEAPOT.

On a bonbon plate
with Martha.

Here hE is in the Window of
an Antiques STORE.

On A Lollipop.

HERe hE is down the BLoCK
fRom my Apartment.

HERE he is
on a TERRACE in ROME.

No, WAit. THAt's my Mother,
SARa. But I think you will
Agree she looked A lot like GEORge.

Who WAS he?
WHAT do we KNOW?
The most famous thing
EVERYONE KNOWS is NOT TRUE.

The CHERRY tree/CAN'T-tELL-A-LIE story is A
FABRICATION by A biograpHER. Though I believe
WASHINGTON WAS A VERY MORAL MAN

who WAS AVERSE to Lying
and partial to cherry pie.

The other thing is TRUE.
HE SUFFERed SO FROM his TEETh —

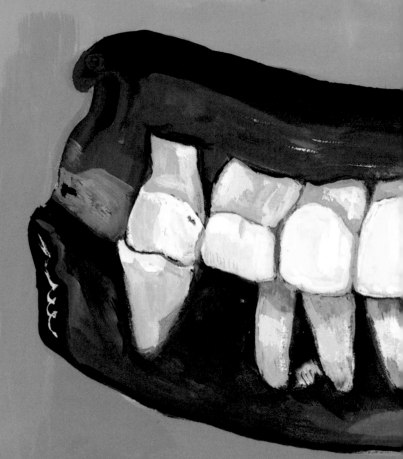

ONE After the otHER being pulled, until
fiNALLy hE WAS LEFt with oNE
SAd Tooth.

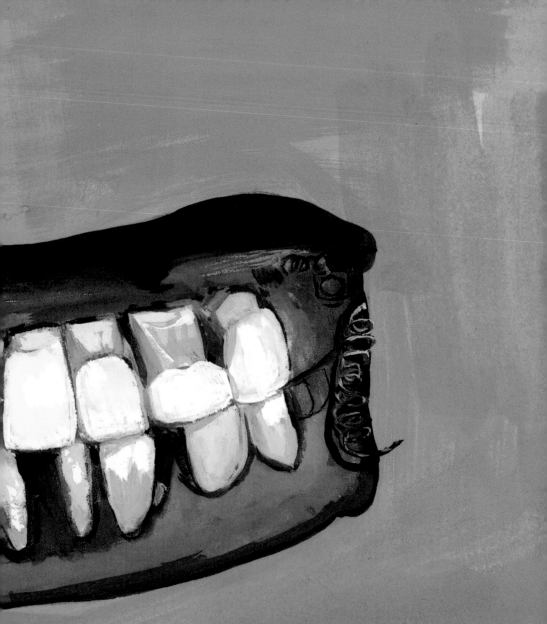

The dentures were heavy — made from Hippopotamus ivory with wire springs. Argh. And they were too BIG. He looked as if he had swollen cheeks.

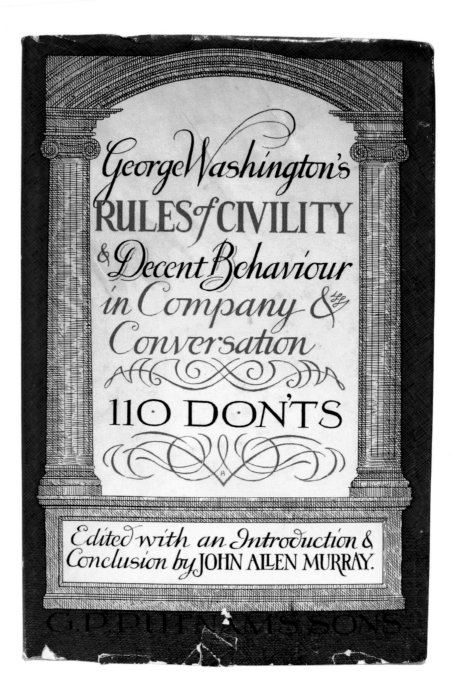

George Washington's
RULES of CIVILITY
& Decent Behaviour
in Company &
Conversation

110 DON'TS

Edited with an Introduction &
Conclusion by JOHN ALLEN MURRAY.

G. P. PUTNAM'S SONS

He Aspired to be A Gentleman and, when he was still A Teenager, wrote "George Washington's Rules of Civility and Decent Behavior in Company and Conversation."

Rule 1. Every Action done in Company ought to Be with Some sign of RESPECT to those that are PRESENT.

Rule 100. Cleanse Not your Teeth with the Tablecloth.

He was a Hero and became Famous at the Age of 22, fighting for the British in the French and Indian War.

⁂

Disillusioned with the British, he became the general of the Continental Army,

LeAding the 13 COLONiES in the FighT for Independence.

HERE is the FLAG that he TOOK
with him into BATTLE.

As he said,
" LET US RAISE A STANDARD
to which the
WISE and HONEST
CAN RepAiR."

✳

WhAT made it POSSiBLE foR
him to PERSEVERE and inspiRE
A RAgTAg ARMY foR six YEARS?
The AMERiCANS BELieved
in thEIR CAUSE.
And thEy hAd HELp.
The FRENch hATed the BRiTish
and cAme to the Aid of the CoLoNiES.

The NoBLE StRUggLE inspiRed the 19-yeaR-old
Marquis de Lafayette (whose family Motto was
"Why Not") to Leave his 16-yeaR-old wife,
Marie AdRieNNE FRANçoise de NoaiLLes

(whom he did indeed Love, hair and all), and joined the CAUSE in AMERICA. WASHINGTON Adored Lafayette

and the feeling WAS ReTURNed. Lafayette named his son GeoRge WASHington!

THERE WAS NO LACK of Affection FOR
LAfayETTE in my FAMily. My parents

admired the Marquis and we
celebrated his BIRthday
every year

with a
Lovely
Lemon Layer Cake.

And GEORGE's PRivate Life.
I go visit Mount VERNON, his home on
a hiLL overLooking the PotoMAC
in VIRgiNia.
He designed and RedesigNed the HousE,
while worKing on designs foR A
NationaL CapitAL City.

The house is Not LARge.
The Rooms aRe spaRe but elegANt.
The COLORS BLASt at you.

NeveR Let it be sAid that AmeRicANs
weRE AfRaid of COLOR.
It wAS A Civilized life. GeoRge and MaRtha
EnteRtAined ConstaNtly.

MARTHA WORE FANCY SHOES. THEY LOVED
each OTHER. MARTHA WOULD JOIN him at WINTER
CAMPS DURING the WAR.

THEY hAd MANY doGS. ONE of thEM WAS NaMEd SWEET LiPS.

WHEN the WAR finally cAme to AN ENd, GeoRge cAme hoME to bE "UNdER the shadow of My owN vinE and My owN fig tREe,"

coNtENt to woRk oN his fARM.
HE WAS an ENTRepENeuR.
SELLing HerRing! RunNing a distiLLeRy.

Building a FLOUR MiLL, which you can

visit toDAY and where you
can buy the CORNMeaL
to Make EXCellent
CORN BRead .

WISE. CAUTIOUS. HE WAS NOT AN intellectual, but he VALUed his LIBRARY.

He was not destined to remain on his estate.

George was revered. He was exalted.

President for eight years, he rejected a third term

and returned to Mount Vernon.

Thomas Jefferson, who later became his ADVERSARY, said there would have been no United States without george Washington.

He had only three years of peace. He died from complications of a cold at the age of 67. And here is the bed he slept in

and died in.

And now.
The chairs on the back porch

Look out on the same view he saw.

We have the Mount Vernon Ladies Association
to thank. Formed in 1853, when the
family could no longer hold on to the estate
(and the Federal government declined to purchase!),
a group of SPLendid women, who
apparently were not
afraid of an extra
helping of
MUTTON
or
BLANcmange,
bought the
Estate to
PReSeRVE
and
Maintain
his
Vision and
Legacy.

444

You can visit the gardens where 300,000 bees produce honey. You can SEE the fig trees laden with figs.
On the wall in the entrance hALL is a KEY FROM the BASTILLE, given to WASHINGTON by LAFayetté in 1790.

It remains where it was placed that DAY.

"Give me LEAVE, my dear GeneraL, to present you ... with the MAIN KEY of the FORTRESS of DESPOTISM. It is a TRIBUTE, which I OWE, AS A SoN to my AdoptivE father, as an aide-de-CAMP to my GeneraL, AS A missionary of Liberty to its PATRiaRcn."

—Marquis de Lafayette

A SHORT VISIT TO the
White House

It was Raining in Washington.
The Ginkgo trees were all Black trunk

and yellow Leaf.

The House Luminous in a gray mist.

And inside, a Burst of Color. Again.

The Red Room.

The GREEN Room, with a Red chair.

And outside — a farm (ALMOST).
The garden has vegetables and fruit
and 60,000 bees making honey.

Washington never lived in this house.
But his image is everywhere. And
Lafayette's as well.

It could be that the current
president and his wife have the
same integrity as the first president
and his wife. Could be.
And I do imagine that, on festive
occasions, the first family will

Celebrate with a Lovely Lemon Layer Cake.

Happiness

It was raining in New York.

The trees were wet and black, and people walked up Fifth Avenue.

WHERE is happiness?
WhAT is happiness?
What did Thomas Jefferson mean?
The pursuit of happiness.
I visit DR. JAMES WATSON.

Maybe there is a genetic explanation
for HAPPINESS.

And ALL we need to do is
TAKE a PILL
that puts it into Action.
I asked him.
He could not tell me because
No one REALLy KNows.
And anyway, everyone has to be
SAd part of the time;
otherwise, you would be INSANe.

I looked at him.
He takes walks. Plays tennis.
He works.
He looks at trees.

Those are good ways to find happiness.
To find peace of mind.

Me? I work. And walk.
And go to museums.

I LOOK at VELÁZQUEZ'S INFANTA.

I Look at a woman in a Red DRESS with a Snappy Hair do
Looking at the Infanta.
Later, I see her going home in HER fur-collared COAT.
NOT the Infanta. the woman.

A present arrives.

It is a book by Vladimir Nabokov,

who is
NO LONGER
ALIVE.

There are so many people I miss.
Oh, Vladimir. Oh, Sara.
Oh, George.
Oh, Marquis de Lafayette.
Where are you all?
This is not a question to ask
if you want to be
Happy.

I clean my house.

I take Napkin-folding classes.

I make plans for trips
to gardens where I will sit
and draw and eat a
meringue and savor the
moment.

Why not?

IN my family
we do not
say "goodbye."
WE SAY
" So LONG."

Cake

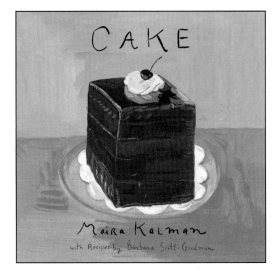

In *Cake*, renowned artist and author Maira Kalman and food writer Barbara Scott-Goodman bring us a beautifully illustrated book dedicated to their mutual love of cakes. Kalman's enchanting illustrations, in her inimitable style, and Scott-Goodman's mouthwatering recipes complement each other perfectly, making *Cake* a joyful whimsical celebration of a timeless dessert.

PP PENGUIN PRESS    PENGUIN BOOKS

Ready to find your next great read? Let us help. Visit prh.com/nextread

BELOVED DOG

Dogs have lessons for us all. In *Beloved Dog*, Maira Kalman illuminates our cherished companions as only she can. From the dogs lovingly illustrated in her acclaimed children's books to the real-life pets who inspire her still, Kalman's *Beloved Dog* is joyful, beautifully illustrated, and, as always, deeply philosophical.

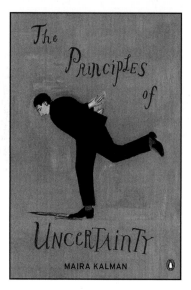

THE PRINCIPLES OF UNCERTAINTY

An irresistible invitation to experience life through a beloved artist's psyche, *The Principles of Uncertainty* is a compilation of Maira Kalman's *New York Times* columns. Part personal narrative, part documentary, part travelogue, part chapbook, and all Kalman, these brilliant, whimsical paintings, ideas, and images—which initially appear random—ultimately form an intricately interconnected worldview, an idiosyncratic inner monologue.

PENGUIN BOOKS